The English Teacher's Handbook

Helena Ceranic

continuum

Continuum Internatinoal Publishing Group
The Tower Building   80 Maiden Lane, Suite 704
11 York Road   New York,
SE1 7NX   NY 10038

www.continuumbooks.com

British Library Cataloguing-in-Publication Data
A catalogue record for this book is available from the British Library.

Library of Congress Cataloging-in-Publication Data
Ceranic, Helena.
    The English teacher's handbook / Helena Ceranic.
        p. cm.
    ISBN 978-1-84706-072-3
    1. English language–Study and teaching (Secondary)–Great Britain–Handbooks, manuals, etc. 2. English teachers–Great Britain–Handbooks, manuals, etc. 3. High school teachers–Great Britain–Handbooks, manuals, etc. I. Title.

    LB1631C4463   2009
    428.0071'241–dc22

                                                          2008047247

Typeset by BookEns Ltd, Royston, Herts.
Printed and bound in Great Britain by MPG Books Ltd, Bodmin, Cornwall

The English Teacher's Handbook

Available from Continuum

100 Ideas for Teaching English -- Angella Cooze
Teaching English 3-11 – Cathy Burnett and Julia Myers
Getting the Buggers to Write: 2nd Edition – Sue Cowley
Getting the Buggers to Read: 2nd Edition – Claire Senior
Encouraging Reading – Susan Elkin

The Handbook Series

The Citizenship Teacher's Handbook – Kate Brown and Stephen Fairbrass
The Mathematics Teacher's Handbook – Mike Ollerton
The Trainee Teacher's Secondary Handbook – Gererd Dixie

Contents

Introduction: The highs and lows of being an English teacher

Like all teaching, teaching English can be at once rewarding and frustrating, creative and confining, inspiring and challenging. Many of us enter the profession to share our love of language, to inspire students to enjoy literature and to develop their communication skills. However, the reality of the job and its workload and associated pressures can prove daunting and disillusioning. The reported demise of reading and literacy levels has caused the spotlight to shift to functional English and basic language skills. In the drive to raise standards in Maths and English, the fun elements of the subject that most of us relish appear to have been sidelined; reading an entire novel with a class, creating poetry and creative writing, or acting out scenes from our favourite Shakespeare plays, can seem indulgent and frivolous unless they explicitly prepare students for the coursework and exams that loom on the horizon. Meanwhile employers continue to complain of poor basic skills and further education institutions blame the current English curriculum for spoon-feeding students and failing to equip them with the tools to read and write for themselves. We also have the challenge of keeping our lessons relevant and engaging among the development of new technologies and media. As English teachers we juggle skill development, subject knowledge and enjoyment in an attempt to please students, parents and school leaders while endeavouring to maintain a sense of job satisfaction. While these challenges exhaust us, they are what keep the job exciting.

As a new English teacher you will be attempting to combine theory with practice; trying to cover the curriculum and tick all the policy boxes while surviving the mind-numbing fatigue that comes from developing whizzy lessons and tackling marking mountains while burning the midnight oil. When you are frazzled and your lengthy to-do list is weighing you down it is easy to become cynical and defeatist or feel tempted to lower your expectations. English teachers adopt a range of coping strategies to survive the demands of the job. The two approaches that can dominate English staffrooms are the 'I want my students to love English, I don't care about results' versus the 'I can get my students good grades by coaching them through coursework and teaching them exam tips'. This handbook is designed to share tried and tested approaches to deal with the difficulties and apparent paradoxes inherent in English teaching without having to undermine your original rationale and motivations for entering the profession. Through a range of practical teaching strategies I demonstrate that it is possible to make English teaching and learning enjoyable without compromising standards; in fact, engaging English lessons actually raise standards.

While English is a rich and diverse discipline with opportunities for personal response and creative composition, the push for standards and curriculum coverage can cause the subject to become dry, dull and utilitarian in approach. Many students themselves tend to adopt a matter-of-fact stance towards their learning, continually questioning the relevance and practical use of lesson content and often desperately seeking the 'right' answer or technique. One of the biggest challenges for English teachers can be to develop expertise and extend independent learning skills. This can often cause a tension between creativity and practicality, for teachers as well as students.

Teaching English across key stages provides variety and a sense of progression but it also involves balancing a range of objectives, texts and assessment criteria. The important thing is to keep focused on the bigger picture – developing students' English skills, subject knowledge and appreciation of language, regardless of age, class or topic. As it is easy to get bogged down in the minutia of photocopying, marking and report writing, this can cause a loss of purpose and priority. It is crucial to maintain your vision of English teaching – avoid losing the idealism and enthusiasm that you doubtless demonstrated at your initial teacher training interview. Many of us enter the profession as a result of inspiring and influential teachers in our own educational experiences; the English teachers that we admire and remember are likely to be those who fuelled our own confidence, interest and passion for the subject. They may have been highly organised and efficient individuals as well, but I doubt that is what made them memorable and effective. The chapters in this book are intended to support your craft of teaching and help you to develop flexible approaches and ideas that you can adapt to suit your teaching style and interests.

Starting out as an English teacher can feel like an isolated experience; despite the fact that the rest of your department, and the rest of the country, is covering the same curriculum, planning for a new topic or text can make you feel like a lone ranger conquering uncharted territory. This book guides you towards a collaborative and confident approach to planning and sourcing resources. While perfectionism is a luxury you can afford when you have five hours available to plan a starter or mark one set of books during your training placement, a full timetable will necessarily cause you to adjust your approach. You may be lucky enough to have excellent faculty schemes of work, complete with accompanying interactive and attractive re-sources, or a no-book-making policy, but in the reality of busy English teaching, it is likely that the quality of departmental lesson plans will range from patchy to non-existent and that assessment can dominate your evenings and weekends. This handbook contains advice for finding, tweaking and creating successful resources and teaching ideas, plus tips for organising them so that you aren't in the frustrating, but all too familiar, position of reinventing the wheel that you know you have lying around somewhere from last year. It also tackles the bane of most English teachers' existence: marking.

Overall, the purpose of this handbook is to help not only balance your workload but reduce it. I advocate strategies to minimise tedium, administration and pointless time-wasting, to enable you to prioritise your time to the enjoyable aspects of the job that will have the biggest impact on students' learning and your own self-fulfilment and enjoyment.

Planning for outstanding English lessons 2

Principles for effective planning

◆ The importance of good planning and why it often gets sidelined

Good planning is at the heart of effective English teaching and learning; it enables us to ensure that students cover the curriculum while making good progress. While experience will help you to develop confidence and a teaching repertoire that will provide planning shortcuts, failing to plan, as the clichéd maxim goes, is planning to fail. Many experienced colleagues may seem to get away with minimal planning and have the 'door handling' technique (deciding what to do as you enter the classroom) down to a fine art, but in reality they are likely to have rehearsed these lessons, or versions of them, on numerous previous occasions. While 'winging it' can occasionally lead to successful, interesting and unique learning outcomes, there is a difference between flexible teaching, risk-taking and wasting learning time. Hoping that learning objectives will be met by happy accident is a risky and irresponsible approach to English teaching but it is understandable why planning can become sidelined. In the hectic fray of marking, report writing and countless other jobs, planning can drop to the bottom of the priority pile perhaps because, unless you are being formally observed, it's the invisible part of the job. Parents, students and Heads of Department will start to notice if you are behind with your marking or if your reports are overdue, but with a measure of confidence and a skill for improvisation no one need ever know that you made up the activities for period three during the drive to school, in the toilets at the end of break, or while taking

5

the register at the start of the lesson. Emergency planning should be restricted to emergencies otherwise you can slip into teaching formulaic, uninspiring lessons that fill time instead of forming a sequence of learning activities that help students to develop their English skills.

◆ Focusing on the bigger picture – not just filling lesson time

It is crucial to locate your lessons within the bigger picture of medium- and long-term learning objectives if you are going to successfully plan for curriculum coverage and progression. Your department should have schemes of work that address National Curriculum criteria; you may even have detailed schemes that offer individual lesson plans. It is important not to lose focus of the main objectives and outcomes for a term, topic or text; it is easy to think of relevant activities to fill lesson time without fully considering what students should be learning and how this links to what they have learnt before and what they will learn in the future. Similarly, be careful not to ignore aspects of departmental schemes of work because the resources aren't appealing at the risk of missing out a crucial part of the English curriculum. An approach that focuses on learning objectives and students' individual needs will help you to plan suitable and relevant lessons.

◆ Addressing learning objectives in your planning (rather than teaching objectives)

In the early stages of your English teaching career you will, quite naturally, be preoccupied with teaching objectives rather than learning objectives. Being new to the theatre of the classroom and the complexities of teaching you will be concerned, first and foremost, with the practicalities of your lessons: What questions will you ask? What resources do you need to prepare? What will you do if little Jonny sabotages your meticulously planned activities...? It is difficult to maintain focus on core learning objectives for a scheme of work while your main objective is to survive the hour. If behaviour and workload dominate a new teacher's priorities, it is easy to slip into planning activities with the main objective of controlling bad behaviour, entertaining students or minimising preparation. As you become more experienced and at ease with standing in front of a group of teenagers, it is imperative that you purposefully plan for learning to take place. This sounds like a very obvious thing to say, but the routine of filling in the lesson pro formas during a training year can make learning objectives meaningless sentences that are merely stated on a form or on the board at the start of a lesson; what is important is how these learning objectives are put into practice and achieved.

◆ Making NC documents work for you

Being a core subject has its advantages; there are a plethora of resources produced by the government, QCA, subject associations and many other organisations to support your planning. In the first tentative months of planning, The National Strategy documents can seem daunting; sheaves of paper crammed full of educational jargon can seem like threatening checklists reminding you of all of the aspects of the subject that you haven't covered, but it is important that you use these documents as tools for the planning process. Unfortunately, the sheer wealth of materials available can be off-putting and time-consuming to sift through, causing you to revert to designing lesson plans and accompanying resources from scratch. However, it's important to familiarise yourself with the English curriculum, framework resources and exam specifications to alleviate the fear factor. Aside from the actual syllabus objectives, the National Curriculum and other core documents do include a range of resources to support students' learning; good teaching ideas can be hidden among text-heavy documents – use indexes to help you source relevant pages. Websites are often easier to navigate. It is worth remembering that these publications have been produced to support the teaching of English and your Head of Department and colleagues should help you to locate key documents and helpful materials.

◆ Focusing on the quality of learning experiences for all

It is crucial to ensure that your planning is appropriate for all of the students in your class; however interesting your activities are, if the level of pace and challenge is not right, then you will fail to engage and sustain the students' interest. When planning, it's more important to focus on *who* you are teaching and what they will learn instead of being preoccupied by *what* you are teaching, otherwise your hours of planning and preparation may be entirely wasted on students that just 'don't get it'.

A teaching strategy or resource that worked really well with a top set the last time you used it will need adapting to suit the needs of a mixed ability group. When time is at a premium, creating differentiated resources can seem impossible to do. However, adapting teaching resources doesn't always have to mean producing a separate worksheet. The way in which you ask questions, expect students to record their ideas or the amount of time you allow for a specific task can be tweaked according to the nature of the class you are teaching.

Traditionally, English teachers have got away with the 'differentiation by outcome' approach. While it is true that open-end tasks such as writing a letter of complaint leave scope for students to respond to the same task and achieve grades ranging from a level 3 to an A*, you will need to consider what kind of preparation a Year 7 class doing it for the first time will need and how this will differ from a Year 11 revision class. It is important to consider how you will support students' learning without making them entirely dependent on adult help throughout the lesson.

◆ *Scope for evaluation – planning for opportunities to gauge teacher and pupils' views*

As a trainee teacher, writing individual lesson evaluations are part of the learning process. Once teaching a full timetable, you are unlikely to review your lessons in such a formal way; however, it is important to remain reflective about your practice in order to improve it. Jotting down notes on your planner at the end of a lesson may be one way to record how particular activities went, but in the frenzy of tracking homework and detentions, collecting in resources and getting ready for the next lesson, this is likely to be impossible. In reality, during a conversation with a colleague over coffee, while tidying your desk at the end of the day or during the drive home from work may be the best time for you to think over your lessons and evaluate what went well and what didn't, and consider why.

Aside from personal reflection, it is also important to capture students' views of lesson activities. You will develop a feel for what has worked and what hasn't, but building in opportunities for students to evaluate learning opportunities will give you more concrete feedback, in addition to anecdotal comments and assumptions. Self and peer evaluation have become common-place in the English classroom – I think it is beneficial to shift the focus to an evaluation of the learning process itself rather than just individual student outcomes. It is empowering for students to feel as though their opinions count, and the vast majority use the opportunity to make thoughtful and mature reflections.

Generating a questionnaire may be a good way to gauge students' views about a lesson, but unless you are seeking quantifiable data I'd advise against conducting formal surveys – they can be time-consuming and laborious to generate, conduct and then analyse the results. I recommend frequent and informal feedback in place or rare and rigorous. Circulating a class and talking to groups and individuals about the task itself, rather than their work, can elicit students' perspectives on the lesson. A simple plenary activity can be asking students to review what they have learnt that lesson and what they found challenging, interesting or easy about the learning activities. This could be a discussion activity or you could ask students to note down their opinions – either option can give you a flavour of students' experience of the lesson. I'd also advocate building in time for a more comprehensive review at the end of a scheme of work; it is interesting to see which lesson activities students can recall – whether with fondness or angst – and what they feel they have learnt. Of course you will get the predictable 'Do less work and watch more videos' suggestions, but you may also find some interesting reflections about the activities. Through an evalua-tion exercise, I discovered that my bottom set year Year 8s enjoyed a scheme of work comparing *Anne Frank's Diary* to *The Princess Diaries*, even though they found the essay difficult. This helped me to realise that, with support, this group were capable of comparative analysis. Many commented that they would have appreciated more time to research Anne Frank's life and context – not something I would have expected to hear. I will build more opportunities for this into the scheme the next time I teach it.

Once you become confident with tapping into student voice in the classroom, you can move from blanket evaluation of lessons and schemes to more focused reflection. The important thing is to keep the evaluation process itself interesting and varied otherwise students will suffer from consultation fatigue.

Long-term planning

◆ *How to be strategic about your planning*

Departmental long-term plans will differ in terms of style and detail but their ostensible function is to ensure appropriate curriculum coverage and pace. A clear and organised long-term plan will help you to keep focused on the main learning outcomes for a specific scheme of work and how they fit into the bigger picture of the students' development in English at secondary school. Long-term plans are often dictated by term length, calendar dates and resource availability. While it is important to consider the practical implications such as how many weeks you have left to prepare Year 11 before their study leave, or how will you manage to read the whole of a novel in a short half-term with only half a class set, it is important not to get bogged down in this at the risk of 'doing' a novel or rushing through designated lesson time. Having explicit learning objectives in long-term plans instead of just curriculum content will help with this.

◆ *Deciding how long to spend on different topics*

If you are fortunate, you will have lots of support and guidance from your faculty about how to utilise your lessons to best effect. There should be scope for flexibility though, depending on the needs of the classes that you are teaching. I would also encourage you to be reflective about the suggested time frames given to texts and topics. For GCSE courses it's worth considering how much each piece of coursework and exam component is worth. It doesn't really make sense working on coursework and neglecting exam skills up until Christmas of Year 11 when more marks rest on students' exam performance. Similarly spending an equal amount of time on a media response based on a two-hour film as a prose essay on a bulky text, when the first is worth 5 per cent of a Language GCSE and the second contributes to 10 per cent of the exam paper, is nonsensical. Try to divide up the year's lessons by keeping focused on the key outcomes and curriculum requirements. Most schools still stick to half-termly schemes of work, but it may be appropriate to break this time down, especially around examination periods. Keep focused on what skills you want students to develop and try, as much as possible, to make links between schemes to promote transferable skills and avoid students' compartmentalising their knowledge.

◆ *Planning for curriculum coverage and variety*

A good long-term plan should provide a range of texts, skills and activities across the course of a year. However, many long-term plans still revolve around content rather than skills. As a class teacher it is likely that you will need to add flesh to the departmental long- and medium-term plans for individual lessons. Ensure that students have the opportunity to develop a range of English skills and work in a variety of contexts during a scheme of work. Build a repertoire of different reading and writing activities to prevent students from continually writing diary entries or letters in role; these are the staple task for English teachers but they don't allow students to develop a range of different skills through exploring various text forms. Consider how much emphasis your lessons place on the different curriculum strands.

- Is speaking and listening given the same weight as reading and writing?
- How do you explicitly teach reading skills and make sure that you aren't always testing comprehension through written responses?
- Is there equality among Key Stages 3 and 4 in term of the pace and enjoyment planned for in lessons?

While students have different learning styles, teachers tend to have their own teaching styles. To succeed in keeping your lessons fresh and engaging avoid falling into a rut of always delivering your lessons in a predictable way. All students benefit from variety.

◆ *Planning for progression*

While developing a familiar repertoire of modelling and planning strategies is comforting for teachers and students, it is always worth reflecting on how you are developing and progressing students' learning skills. For example, what skills are you teaching in Year 7 that will enable students to be proficient essay writers by the time they are in Year 11? How are the speaking and listening presentation skills you introduce at the start of Key Stage 3 built upon and developed to allow students to be confident speakers during their GCSE tasks and beyond?

Progression tools are available through strategy materials to allow you to plan skills by year group. However, it's worth remembering that it isn't always appropriate to stick to age-determined objectives. If a Year 8 student is already demonstrating many of the skills expected by the end of Key Stage 4, it wouldn't make sense to limit them to objectives designed for their age group. Getting a good grasp of your students' strengths and areas for development should help you to plan activities that will provide appropriate challenges and that will lead to progress in your lessons; as will maintaining a good sense of how tasks link to past and future activities. If you set students very specific targets after a piece of work, are they given the opportunity to put these into practice?

Medium term planning

◆ Planning an effective sequence of lessons

Departmental schemes of work should provide you with medium-term plans that explicitly outline learning objectives and key outcomes. More detailed schemes may also include individual lesson plans. Regardless of the format and style of your departmental planning, it is crucial that you have a clear sense of how individual lessons fit into the medium-term plan. Even if you have strong schemes to follow, it is crucial that you read them through fully before you start teaching individual lessons so that you have a clear understanding of the learning objectives and tasks. If you merely look at the next lesson on the scheme just before you teach it, your delivery is likely to lack suitable direction, pace and organisation. Before starting to teach a scheme, it's important to prioritise outcomes and activities, plan for differentiation and prepare/locate/book necessary resources in advance. Once you have a good idea of how the whole scheme is going to be delivered, I would recommend planning three lessons at a time; this prepares you for the week ahead and ensures progression without being stifling. Some highly-organised teachers may wish to fill their planners with lesson details a term in advance but this leaves very little scope for flexibility within the scheme – once you start teaching it you may wish to cut out activities or add extra ones that you hadn't thought of at the start.

◆ *Writing a successful scheme of work – keeping focused on learning goals and the bigger picture*

If your department does not have detailed schemes of work including individual lesson plans, I recommend that you start to create your own; not only will this curry favour with colleagues but it will help you to plan systematically and will drastically cut down on your workload for the following year. When starting to design a scheme of work it's important to keep the learning objectives central and keep focused on some important questions:

> – *What skills do you want the students to learn or develop in the scheme?*
> – *What kinds of texts, contexts and forms do you want them to explore?*
> – *What types of learning activities will allow students to achieve these objectives?*
> – *How will you measure their learning – what types of outcomes and assessment activities will you include?*

I recommend creating a front sheet for your scheme of work that includes all of this important information – from that you can start to think of suitable lesson content by drawing on personal experience, resources that you have discovered and suggestions from colleagues. However, it's important to keep focused on your learning objectives during this planning process, otherwise you might get carried away with seemingly fun teaching ideas that have nothing to do with the original purpose of your scheme.

◆ *Planning for variety*

A successful scheme of work will include pace and variety to keep you and the students engaged and motivated. The types of lesson activities and outcomes should appeal to a variety of learning styles and should allow you to observe the students learning in a range of formats. Watch out for repetitive and predictable lesson formats: you may resort to starting every lesson with a brainstorm activity and ending it with peer evaluation but this will become tedious and prevent students from developing a range of learning skills. Similarly, when teaching a novel it might be tempting to fill the main body of the lesson with reading and writing chapter summaries or cloze exercises. Spending a bit more time thinking, before committing

your teaching activities to paper or screen, may allow you to develop more varied and creative approaches. I also recommend that you are mindful of the balance of individual-, group- and teacher-led tasks: many new English teachers exhaust themselves, their voices and their students by dominating lessons with lecturing or entertaining students from the front of the classroom. It's important that you plan for independent learning time that will allow you to circulate the class to support individual students.

◆ Building in useful homework activities

The best time to plan homework is when you are writing a scheme of work, then the activities can be embedded into the learning process rather than being an after-thought. Most schools do have homework policies dictating how much time should be spent on homework per subject per week – use this as a benchmark for how frequently to include homework tasks in your planning (once a week normally works best). Try to ensure that homework activities do follow on from, or prepare students for, work that they will be doing in lesson time to make it relevant and meaningful. Also try to make homework tasks manageable and interesting so that students are motivated to do them. If students know that their homework is taken seriously and that they will be rewarded for it, then they are also more likely to put the effort in.

For research-style homework, I suggest giving a framework or success criteria to prevent them from completing the bare minimum. For GCSE students, context quiz sheets have been successful – I award a certain number of points depending on the difficulty of each question (for example, based on the social, historical and biographical background of Arthur Miller or Mary Shelley). I would also recommend that you provide tasks that allow students an element of choice and creativity. Some popular tasks I have recently set for Year 7 based on the novel *Millions* by Frank Cottrell Boyce including creating an estate agents' advert for their own house or imaginary hermitage; producing a wanted poster; creating a shopping list for spending a million pounds and writing a recipe for being excellent. These activities provided very different and interesting responses that were great for putting on display. While I recommend building in time into the lesson to prepare students for a homework task, e.g. five minutes to discuss or plan what they are going to do, I would avoid setting 'finishing off' homework tasks; students may rush through a task to avoid having to do any work at home, it can also make it seem like a punishment rather than a discrete activity to develop their independent learning skills.

Short-term planning

◆ *Outstanding one-off lessons*

In order to satisfy the Ofsted criteria for an outstanding lesson there needs to be evidence of 'exceptional enjoyment and progress of the learners'. Planning a sequence of activities that include the elements below will help you to achieve this, but it is worth remembering that your relationship with a class and your capacity to have an outstanding lesson with your students rests on good learning, behaviour, and assessment practices, all things that take time to develop and embed.

Variety:	Have you included a range of different activities within the lesson?
	Will they appeal to different learning styles?
	Do they differ from the types of tasks that were included in their last lesson?
Pace:	How much time will you give to certain activities to sustain interest and momentum in the lesson?
	Is it crucial for all students to complete every task that you give them?
	What can students who finish early move on to?
Challenge:	How do the activities build on the skills and knowledge that the students already have?
	How will you ensure that all students in the class can access the learning and be stretched by it?
Trust:	How will you organise the lesson to make students feel comfortable and safe when contributing to the lesson?
	How do you plan to interact with the students during the lesson?
Confident:	How will you ensure that your subject knowledge and classroom organisation is secure?
Engagement:	How are you going to capture the interest and motivation of the students?
	What kinds of stimulus will you include to spark their thinking or imagination?

Clarity:	How are you going to be explicit about your learning objectives and expectations?
	How will these be communicated to the students?
Organisation:	How will you manage the lesson effectively?
	How many resources do you need to use and how will these be organised?
	How are you going to deploy the skills of the adults and students in the class?

◆ Focusing on the learning taking place – how students will learn, not what will they do

It is possible to plan a lesson that meets all of the requirements above without students actually learning anything. It is easy to fall into the trap of judging an effective lesson by how engaged and busy students appear to be. However, the questions you always need to keep in the forefront of your mind when planning a lesson is 'What do I want the students to learn?' and 'How will this learning take place?' This is more than just a change of emphasis in the vocabulary that you use in your planning: some teachers use the language of learning in lesson objectives and yet the lesson plan still revolves around what students will be *doing*.

Once you have a clear sense of the learning objectives you want to cover in a lesson, make sure that you keep these in mind while you are planning lesson activities and preparing resources to support them. For example, if you wish students to explore possible meanings and messages in poetry, you need to plan for exploratory learning to take place. This may involve building in time for group discussion, providing stimulus to accompany the poems or giving prompts to develop personal interpretation. Conversely, simply handing out a copy of the poem and getting students to work through a series of comprehension-style questions in silence is unlikely to achieve the learning objective you set out with.

◆ Planning for effective interaction and questions in the classroom

Question and answer sessions are a staple of the English classroom. Many English teachers use Q&A throughout lessons, most prominently during starters, to gauge or recall prior learning, and during feedback or plenary sessions to share understanding and ideas. Like any other teaching resource, it is important that the quality and relevance of questions is considered. While good questioning has the potential to stimulate thought, generate ideas and embed understanding, poor questioning can actually be demotivating and counterproductive.

When teaching your first few lessons as a trainee teacher it is likely that you prepared a script of questions in advance. As you gain confidence in your English teaching and interactions with students you are more likely to improvise your questions according to the flow and content of the lesson. Nevertheless, it is still worth being self-conscious about the style of questions you are using and how this technique is being developed in your lesson. Quick-fire, whole-class Q&A may be effective to generate pace and interest at the start of a lesson but this format will become tiresome, especially for those students who are reluctant to share their understanding in front of the whole class or struggle to recall information at speed. Consider the purpose of the questions before deciding what type of questions to use.

Building in thinking time or discussion time around important questions will help students to engage properly with the task rather than rush to answer or leave someone else to do it. This will also enable you to circle the class and use the 'no hands up' rule, knowing that every student has been given a chance to practise their response already. While you may start with some simple closed questions, you should plan to extend and challenge students by using open questions, not only in whole-class, but during one-to-one discussion and within the lesson activities themselves. This will promote more expansive thinking and personalised responses.

Emergency planning

◆ *Emergency lesson ideas*

Even if you are the most organised of teachers you will find yourself planning a lesson at the very last minute at some point or another. You may even have to scrap or modify a lesson you had already planned because of a change of circumstances (you've lost your voice; sports day has been cancelled; Year 7 are hyper after a wet and windy lunch break and won't cope with the drama lesson that you had planned).

Ideally, a scheme of work should include some stand-alone lesson ideas that could be used in emergencies. A self-explanatory and straightforward worksheet that students can complete by themselves that will not have been covered in the usual scheme is a god-send when you need to set up an emergency cover lesson. There are plenty of resources available on websites, such as 'Teachit' that could be used in this way. If your department has a set of textbooks, you may also be able to find some appropriate activities that can be earmarked for this purpose.

Having some tried and tested generic resources up your sleeve that can be adapted for different year groups and activities is also a good idea. For example, laminated pictures of different holiday locations could be used as stimulus for a piece of descriptive writing or poetry, or they could form the basis of a piece of persuasive writing or travel-writing task. Some of the best emergency lessons are one-offs that have nothing to do with what students have been studying, but I would recommend trying to plan something that is loosely linked to previous work, otherwise students may question the relevance of what they are being asked to do.

◆ Tips for setting effective cover work

Teachers often complain that setting cover work is more of a nuisance than actually delivering a lesson themselves, which explains why some colleagues never take days off, regardless of how ill they feel. However, there are some strategies to cut down on the time spent preparing work, to minimise the hassle for the cover teacher and the time you spend clearing up when you get back:

- Set up a cover template in Word and include space for lesson details including referral classrooms, homework and resources. Make sure that this is stuck securely to your desk and leave a spare copy with your Head of Department and, if appropriate, with a colleague in the classroom next door.
- Use post-it notes to label work on your desk (e.g. what class and period the worksheets are for), to avoid any confusion.
- Set clear and simple instructions that non-specialist staff will be able to understand – if students need more detailed information, provide this on a handout rather than expecting the cover teacher to write copious amounts of detail on the board.
- Set a range of activities so that students don't run out of things to do.

- Supply cover staff with a group list and seating plan – these help enormously with classroom management.
- Keep worksheets minimal to avoid coming back to a mountain of muddled up papers that you need to file and sort.
- If you want resources collected back at the end/books handed in/a note of where the class got to… make sure that you request this information explicitly in your cover notes.
- If you are setting cover work from home in the morning, be extra simplistic and try to set work that doesn't need resources, unless they are ready on your desk. Avoid asking your colleagues to root around for materials and do photocopying for you – mornings are frantic enough and they may not have the time.
- Avoid setting cover such as watching a film, finishing something off or drawing pictures. Students are often dismissive of cover lessons and will attempt to turn them into a social break. It's important that you take cover work seriously and set appropriate tasks to give students the message that you expect them to work hard in their English lessons, whether you are there or not.
- Follow up cover work when you get back to school, either by asking students to share what they have done with you, or by marking the outcomes. If students have completed cover work on paper, get them to stick it into their exercise books; this is another way of showing that you value the work that they have done while you weren't there.
- Say thank you to the colleague that took your lesson at the bottom of your cover sheet, and in person, if possible.

◆ *Seasonal lesson ideas – avoiding death by video*

At the end of term a lot of teachers resort to showing videos to their classes; teachers are exhausted and students are desperate for 'fun' lessons so it's tempting to succumb to their requests. While it's entirely appropriate to save the film adaptation of a text that you have been studying as a treat to show in the last lesson before the Christmas holidays, this is different from showing whatever DVD you happen to have in your cupboard to fill lesson time and keep students quiet.

As you know, headteachers are inundated with parental requests to take their children on holiday before the end of term; if students aren't actually learning anything in last week of term, then it makes it difficult for us to argue that it's imperative for students to attend school. It is possible to make your end-of-term lessons a bit more fun than usual while still ensuring that learning is taking place. I try to make sure that the last few lessons in a scheme of work approaching the end of the Christmas, Easter or Summer allow for something a bit more creative; they might provide students to work on a collaborative project or an individual design task – something that gives them a bit more freedom but is still relevant and appropriate to what you have been studying.

Departments such as Maths and Modern Foreign Languages are often a good example of how to incorporate seasonal teaching ideas and practical lesson activities into end-of-term lessons. If you do wish to show 'A Muppets' Christmas Carol' because it ties in nicely with your work on Dickens, make sure that you incorporate the text like you would any other; avoid playing the film for the whole hour, build in questions and other activities to make sure that students are engaging with the film, thinking and learning while they are watching, rather than just being a passive audience.

Being organised with your planning

◆ *Planning formats and templates – choose a style that works for you*

Getting your first teacher planner can be a momentous and daunting experience: hundreds of blank pages waiting for you to write all over them. Teachers have different preferences about the style of teacher planner when it comes to ordering one – A4, A5, comb-bound, folder… Whatever format of commercial planner you go for, most will offer you five or six blank rigid boxes per page. You may find this quite restrictive – trying to squeeze copious notes into a small space until they overspill into the next lesson or become illegible. Some teachers resort to using their planner as a diary with minimal lesson notes, either because they plan their lessons in more detail elsewhere or rely on the plans in their head.

A number of my colleagues have opted for electronic planning in place of handwritten notes in a planner. By creating a similar template on the computer you can make boxes as big as you need them to be and print off in draft format to save ink. Most teachers throw away their conventional paper planner at the end of the year even though they will be teaching similar lesson content the following year. The day-to-day format of a planner makes it difficult to track continuity and a series of lesson content, but if you have planned electronically you can copy and paste planning notes and save them for future reference.

If you have good quality schemes of work with short-term lesson plans, copying notes from the scheme of work into your planner page may prove counterproductive. You may find it useful to annotate and modify a copy of the scheme, either by hand or electronically.

◆ *Paper-free planning – avoiding death by worksheet*

A typical English office is full of filing cabinets and folders crammed with worksheets, many outdated and no longer useful. You may have experienced the frustration of searching for a resource that has not been returned to its home and you are likely to be familiar with an overwhelming pile of paper on your desk that needs sorting out at the end of a school day. Unless you are amazingly efficient, filing can become unmanageable and looking for resources can waste a lot of time.

If you have paper resources with no electronic master copy, I would recommend putting a coloured dot in the corner of the worksheet or copying it on to a pastel colour so that you have a master copy that looks different – this will prevent you from giving your last sheet to a student or colleague by accident. If you have made a resource yourself or have been given an electronic copy, save it in a sensible filing system on your computer and then you won't have to worry about filing a paper version. If you have class sets of a worksheet, then try to keep them together and put them into a plastic wallet as soon as you have finished with them; even if you don't get time to file them straightaway, at least they will be kept neat and all together.

Before you print out and photocopy a resource, consider whether it is necessary for students to have a paper copy.

- Could you project the information on to the board for students to read?
- Do they need one each to keep for reference in their books?
- Could they share in pairs or groups to minimise photocopying?

At the end of the lesson consider whether it is important to keep spare copies for next lesson, absent students or to use next time you teach that lesson, or whether it is less hassle to put them in the recycling bin.

◆ *Using ICT to support planning*

Having all resources and schemes of work stored electronically saves a huge amount of time and effort searching for things. If you have access to these files on your laptop, memory stick or by remote access from home, it also means that you don't have to stay at school to complete your planning. If your department hasn't already got one, I would recommend setting up an electronic filing system in which to store all resources in a systematic way. Ideally this would be in a school network area that can be made available offline. Many teachers store resources in their own document areas but this makes sharing more difficult and is unlikely to have the protection of back up that school networks often have.

Having lots of subfolders to organise resources by year group, topic and teacher will make it easier to source relevant resources – it is also important that you save resources with clear and logical names so that you and others can make sense of document titles. Creating hyperlinks from your desktops to regularly-used resource folders each half term will also help you to save time locating materials. Once you have found a useful resource website, bookmark it as a 'favourite' in Internet Explorer for quick and easy access to relevant web pages.

Joint planning

◆ *Planning and sharing with others*

Despite the fact that a department of English teachers are likely to be planning for the same learning outcomes in any given week, planning is often a very isolated experience. I would recommend pairing up with teachers in your team that teach parallel classes so that you can share ideas and resources and cut down on preparation time. When embarking on a new topic or text try to work collaboratively to develop a scheme of work – it will help to bounce ideas off someone else. You are likely to find colleagues in your team who you work well with, perhaps because of a similar approach; it is good to get into practice of exchanging resources with them. While putting a copy of a tried-and-tested resource in their pigeon hole is likely to be gratefully received, it could just end up with a pile of resources to file. E-mail resources instead so that colleagues can save them somewhere safe, or even better, save new resources somewhere centrally accessible so that you get into the habit of reviewing and borrowing each others' materials.

Tips for shared classes

Split classes can be problematic; if you share a class with a colleague you are necessarily going to have to share not only lessons but report writing, parents' evening appointments, scheme of work content, assessment and exam marking. It is best to agree on responsibilities and communication practices at the start of the term to avoid unfair workload balance, duplication, or confusion, later on in the year.

If you are teaching a one-off lesson per fortnight, it is best for the main teacher to set the work and let you know what they want you to cover in that time. However, having to catch up with them before each lesson to get instructions and resources, may prove problematic. It might be best to agree a focus for your lessons for the entire term, e.g. grammar exercises, exam techniques or private reading so that you can prepare and deliver your lessons independently.

If you share a class equally with a colleague, this can be more challenging; you still have to cover the syllabus content, so it will be necessary to split schemes of work. It may be tempting to cover a term's topics between you, for example with one of you delivering the first half term's scheme, e.g. poetry for a whole term, and the other covering the second half term's scheme, e.g. a novel. This allows you to ensure coverage while keeping a clear sense of your own responsibilities. However, as students' timetables are already fragmented into ten or so different subjects a week it may be confusing and unhelpful for them to be studying two different topics in English simultaneously. I would recommend sharing a scheme but agreeing on responsibilities for certain outcomes. For example, one teacher may focus on the speaking and listening project within a scheme while the other delivers the lessons leading up to a piece of fiction writing. While this will involve changing the order of the original scheme and perhaps modifying the content, the students will benefit from being able to make links between their English lessons without teachers having to consult each other between each lesson.

◆ *Team-teaching tips*

You may be fortunate enough to have the opportunity to team-teach in your timetable. Collaborative teaching can help colleagues to learn teaching techniques from each other, and students ultimately benefit from having more than one teacher in their lessons. As with all shared classes, it's important that you have a clear sense of your roles to avoid duplicated efforts, frustration or confusion. It is important that you pair up to do medium-term planning and then agree on specific roles. I recommend taking it in turns to prepare resources and be responsible for delivering lesson content, otherwise the workload may become skewed or you might feel as though you are competing with each other in front of the students. It works well if one of you has the role of a teaching assistant rather than both of you doing a double-act at the front of the classroom for the duration of the lesson.

Sourcing resources

◆ *Being a magpie*

As English teachers rarely rely on textbooks, we are constantly searching for and making resources. In the early stages of your teaching career you will feel the compulsion to make all your worksheets from scratch in the naïve belief that the resource you need either doesn't exist yet or does, but does not meet your exacting standards. Effective English teachers soon begin to realise the benefits of sourcing resources from other colleagues to save time and make friends. In every department that you train or work in, make an effort to share successful resources. Even if you are just visiting another English department for the day, take a memory stick with you and try to get copies of anything that looks interesting. Most teachers are happy to oblige, especially if you return the favour.

I would also strongly recommend investing time into investigating online materials to support the English syllabus, plus other recommended publications and reputable websites, for appropriate teaching ideas. Experienced colleagues will be able to share tried-and-tested sources with you. A number of local authorities and schools have excellent websites where they post resources that you can download.

As an English teacher, potential resources are all around us.

Doctors' surgeries and tourist offices are great places for picking up colourful, glossy leaflets. Tear adverts out of used magazines, and collect the junk mail that comes through your letter box. All these materials make great resources for non-fiction or media analysis purposes. If you get a regular newspaper, look out for good articles that will provoke discussion and debate.

◆ Being discriminatory about resource

While it's good to borrow and file resources to save yourself time and energy, make sure that you review materials periodically to check that they are not tired or outdated. If students are given photocopies that are difficult to read, uninspiring worksheets that were clearly produced decades ago, or tired, tatty, ripped or graffited resources, they are unlikely to be motivated by them or to take care of them themselves.

◆ Tips for tweaking and recycling resources

Rather than starting from scratch, try bringing a tired resource up-to-date by adding a picture or changing the font size or style. Scanning the original resource or manually cutting and pasting the bits that you want can help to modify resources.

Creative planning

◆ Using unconventional materials

It is worth remembering that resources don't have to be limited to worksheets, textbooks or interactive whiteboard files. With a little thought you can accrue imaginative materials for effective stimuli. The internet is a great source for video and music clips. I recommend using songs that relate to topics that you are studying or to accompany the study of poetry. Some of my favourite tangible resources include cotton wool balls for a metaphor starter activity; rope and roses for imagery association; swatches of sari fabric to explore cultural associations and summer ingredients, such as sand and strawberries, to stimulate descriptive writing. Chocolate is another popular resource! By appealing to a range of senses you will engage a variety of learning styles and create memorable lessons. Many of these materials are also cheaper than the photocopying costs of a class set of A4 worksheets.

◆ *Tips for creating new resources*

When creating a new resource, either a worksheet or a file to be projected, consider the following advice:

- Make headings and important reminders larger and bolder than the rest of the text – make sure that the font size is large enough, especially if you are projecting a resource to the whole class.
- Include a good balance of text, images and diagrams.
- Use text boxes to separate information in a clear and logical way.
- Avoid cramming too much information on to a slide/sheet – use relevant images to trigger associations instead of typing everything up.
- Plan for interactivity – how will the resource make students think for themselves rather than just informing or instructing? If you plan for students to keep the resource, consider including questions, gaps to be filled or spaces for annotation.
- Use colours to grab attention but stick to a definite colour scheme to avoid making the resource too chaotic (photocopying costs may prevent this but make the master copy in colour if you are able to project the resource).
- Choose an appropriate font for the subject matter of your resource; a gothic style for a Frankenstein resource adds to the impact. Teachers tend to have their favourites but this can make all of their resources look the same, regardless of topic.

◆ *Planned risk taking*

Some of the best English lessons involve trying something a bit different. New teachers tend to fall into two camps: play it safe by planning straightforward tasks that you know will work, or plan something whacky and hope you can pull it off. To keep yourself and your students engaged, motivated and sane, I would recommend a combination of the two approaches. While students benefit from a routine and the security of clear and prescriptive instructions, they can easily become bored, passive or rebellious if tasks require little personal thought, imagination or challenge.

Try to plan different activities with all of your classes; regardless or age, behaviour or ability. It is easy to fall into planning routines with certain groups of students – consider whether the quality of your planning differs across the classes that you teach. Do you rely on lecture-style delivery with older students, top sets and poorly-behaved classes? Do you plan whizzy lessons for Key Stage 3, low-ability classes or groups with a poor attention span? Does your style of planning depend on how much you enjoy teaching that particular topic? Remember that all groups benefit from a variety of approaches and it is our responsibility to build students' capacity to learn independently.

Calculated risk-taking may involve trying out a group-work, drama, or speaking and listening activity with a boisterous set that you do not trust to behave. While the risk of increased noise, off-task talk and students getting out of their seats may scare you, if the task is properly planned, it is likely that these sorts of pupils will excel, given the opportunity to speak out and put their energy to good use. Tips for making it work:

- Set up a task that the students are interested in and enthused about – they are much more likely to stay focused and on-task if they actually want to do what they have been asked to.
- Prepare students well by giving them the information and instructions they need before splitting them up into groups so that you aren't trying to shout over them.
- Set up the groups yourself in advance to avoid time-wasting and squabbles. Students will ask to swap to be with their friends but if the group lists are typed out, membership appears more rigid. Having a hard copy to place on desks can also be used for noting down individual responsibilities. Once you become more confident with a class, you may trust them to choose their own groups.
- Give out packs or notes on the board that students can refer to during the activity – this will minimise the extent to which you have to repeat instructions to individual groups.
- Accept that noise levels will rise – a classroom full of debate probably has more learning going on than a silent one. However, have ground-rules about volume so that students are able to concentrate – reminders may be necessary.
- Have a recognisable cue that signals to students that you want their attention (buzzer, bell, voice, hand in the air).
- Give clear timings so that students know how long they have left – this also helps to increase pace and focus.
- Allow students flexibility if they consider an approach that is better than the one you planned.

Personalising your planning

◆ Adapting existing schemes and resources

Even if you are fortunate enough to work in a department with comprehensive schemes of work and accompanying resources, you will need to modify these to suit the needs of your class. This may involve switching activities around, adding extra tasks or changing those that will be too easy or too difficult. It will also include improving methods or resources. Some teachers are scared of this, fearing that they will be told off for not sticking to the scheme. I'd advise speaking to your Head of Department to check what the expectations are, but in all likeliness they will be keen for you to personalise the existing plans.

Most departments are in a continual process of updating and improving schemes of work and will welcome the improvements and additions that you make. I would always recommend making a note of the ways in which you have tweaked and adapted a scheme – not only will this be a useful *aide-memoire* for you, but it may help with departmental evaluations and improvements.

◆ Differentiation and extension activities – personalising planning for interests, not just ability

While English teachers are fully aware of the need to differentiate their teaching in order to stretch and support the full range of students within their class, a lack of time and know-how often prevents this from happening effectively. Keeping focused on the students that you teach while planning a sequence of activities will help you to realise what parts of the lesson will need additional support frameworks or challenge. Rather than setting the same tasks for all ability groups, knowing that some will struggle and others will fly through and need additional tasks at the end, try to modify the original task to suit the needs of the students. Mixed-ability groups, in particular, will benefit from being given a range of activities to choose from, differing in difficulty, learning style, degree of independence or format of outcome.

It is also worth considering the interests of the group you teach when modifying a task or resource. Changing a topic to a hobby that interests them or relating it to something topical that they will be keen to discuss will help to engage students.

◆ *Being sensitive to timetable factors*

When planning your lessons for the week, it's important to consider the impact that the timing of your lesson will have on the suitability of the tasks that you have planned. If your lesson is after lunch when students may be hyperactive or tired, after PE when students may trickle in gradually after changing, or following an assembly which includes information that they all want to talk about, is likely to affect not only how your lesson starts, but the demeanour of the students and how they will engage with the tasks you have planned.

You can account for some of these factors in advance; for example setting up an activity that students can start as soon as they enter the room, instead of waiting for the whole class to arrive, before beginning your lesson. However, it's not always possible to anticipate the mood students will be in, so you will need to be perceptive, to sense when there's a need to be flexible with your lesson plan. For example, you may wish to start off with some class reading to settle a group before introducing a whizzy starter activity. Alternatively, if students arrive lethargic, you might improvise a drama warm-up or quiz to get them stimulated and engaged.

Teaching outstanding English lessons

3

Principles for effective teaching

◆ The relationship between teaching and learning

When wrapped up in planning or delivering a good lesson, it's easy to forget that what and how the students are learning is more important that anything else. Good planning will help to ensure that learning objectives can be met through the lesson activities, but the way in which the lesson is delivered determines whether this happens in practice; students will need to be motivated to engage with the activities. However, an all-singing, all-dancing lesson, however entertaining, will not necessarily achieve the desired learning outcomes. It is also important that students are clear about what they are being asked to do; often poor instructions and a lack of explanation can cause a good lesson activity to fall flat on its face because students just didn't 'get it'. Learning objectives should be central to the entire lesson, not just reduced to sentences that are introduced at the start of the lesson, and perhaps revisited at the end. If teachers are focused on the learning process, rather than the outcomes, then students are more likely to understand the rationale behind what they are being asked to do.

◆ Developing a climate for learning

In order for students to be able to engage fully with lesson activities, there needs to be a good learning atmosphere. At a basic level, the conditions of the classroom need to be conducive to learning; extreme temperatures, excessive noise or sunlight shining on the board, all impede students' ability to focus, so try to acknowledge and rectify these issues.

The learning atmosphere is also dictated by the kinds of values and behaviours that are exhibited in your classroom. If a teacher habitually humiliates students or picks on them, this can create a climate in which students are reluctant to expose themselves in fear of embarrassment. Similarly, if certain students tend to dominate classroom discussion, it may become difficult for others to get involved. An optimum learning environment is one in which students feel safe to contribute and where all ideas are valued. Students need to be able to take risks and learn from their mistakes if they are going to develop their knowledge and skills; for English teaching in particular it's important to foster this confidence in students so that they are able to offer a range of responses, not just the ones they think are 'right'.

◆ *Effective classroom management*

Teachers, students and parents all acknowledge that effective classroom management is a crucial element of good teaching. Without students' concentration and focus, learning is difficult to achieve – it is the teachers' responsibility to make sure that students' behaviour is dealt with so that it doesn't impinge on the learning. For new teachers this aspect of the job can be the most daunting, challenging and frustrating. If you teach a difficult class who you struggle to control, regardless of the endless strategies that you have tried, you are likely to feel despondent and helpless. Unfortunately, the struggle to develop your own effective classroom management strategies can be a long one; there is often no quick-fix solution. Consulting colleagues or textbooks is a good way to gain tips and new approaches, but only the experience of being in the classroom and interacting with different types of student behaviour will really give you the confidence to choose appropriate strategies effectively.

Confidence, sensitivity and calmness are the most important qualities to develop – students want to know where they stand with you but it's important that you appreciate the range of factors that will affect how individual students will behave and respond to you. It's really important not to take things personally or lose your composure – this only serves to further knock your confidence and lose respect from your students.

A clear system of sanctions and rewards that are applied consistently will help students to understand your high expectations for behaviour. Just make sure your rules have good learning as the main rationale so that students can appreciate the logic behind your punishments. Also avoid making English work form a part of a punishment; it is reasonable to get students to write incomplete homework during a detention, but be wary of setting students a reading or writing exercise as punishment – this sends out the message that English is not enjoyable. Making children write in silence or listen to you shouting at them will be little incentive to change their behaviour the following lesson. Communication is the best way to come to new understandings about behaviour. I would recommend spending a detention having a proper dialogue with a student to understand their motivations and agree on targets for future lessons. It is important to focus on the impact that their behaviour is having on their own learning and the learning of others, and to make sure that they understand the consequences if they choose to cause further disruption. Ensure that you utilise support systems and ask colleagues for help or advice – it's not admitting defeat, it's making use of others' experience and responsibilities.

◆ Developing students' expertise

'Independent learning' is a phrase that is regularly banded about by teachers but it's important to recognise the difference between independent learning and students doing things on their own. If students are completing simple tasks without much cognitive challenge then arguably they are learning very little from the experience.

One of our core purposes as teachers is to develop students' capacity for life-long learning; to learn how to learn and adapt their skills. While breaking up tasks into manageable chunks is a useful strategy for making work accessible, maintaining pace and keeping students engaged, it can render students de-skilled and overly reliant on teacher instruction. It is important that you plan opportunities to develop thinking skills and independent problem solving so that students are able to learn for themselves.

In a standards-obsessed culture it may be tempting to resort to spoon-feeding students the knowledge and the skills they need to succeed in their examinations – students and parents may well expect this – but learning by rote does little to promote independent thought and will therefore prevent students from achieving high grades in the exams and limit their ability to apply their learning to new situations in the future. As English teachers, we have lots of scope for developing active, inquiring students rather than passive accepting ones; we should take advantage of the debate and independent thought that the subject promotes.

Organising the learning environment

◆ *Organising your learning space*

If you are lucky enough to have your own classroom, then you can really have an impact on the way in which you set up the learning space. If you share a base with another teacher, you may not have the means to ensure that the room is inviting and tidy, but it is always worth talking to the class teacher to arrange a storage or display space of your own if you are in the room on a regular basis.

Displays not only brighten up a dull classroom, they are also a great way of celebrating success and recognising students' achievements. If students know that homework will be selected for display, it gives them a real audience and incentive to work towards. To prevent displays from becoming innocuous wall-paper it's important to update them with current work. Support staff should be available to help you do this; finding keen students with nothing to do at lunchtime is also a good idea. Displays are worth a spending a little bit of thought on, especially if you are going to be looking at them for a few months. Make the extra effort to get work backed so that it looks professional and attractive. Also, have clear eye-catching headings so that students and visitors know what they are looking at. Having students' names and year groups displayed also helps to acknowledge the contributors. Once displays begin to look tired and tatty, try to replace or refresh them so that your classroom continues to look neat and students are not tempted to vandalise them.

The positioning of desks will largely depend on the layout of the classroom. The traditional format of rows assumes that attention needs to be predominately at the front of the class. If you have the space to line the desks in columns with spaces in between, this allows for greater access to individual students. I would recommend this set up at the start of the year as it's easier to command students' attention. If your lessons are characterised by group work and discussion, you may prefer to group tables in clusters; try to angle them so that you don't have students with their backs to you. Some English teachers arrange a horse-shoe-shaped, forum style formation of desks to prompt discussion and debate. While there is scope for changing desks around according to the nature of the planned activity, I would recommend having a default desk arrangement so that students can get settled quickly at the start of a lesson.

◆ Tips for arranging seating and group work

I would advise creating seating plans for all of your classes (perhaps with the exception of A Level groups), especially at the start of the year. It helps you to learn students' names more quickly as you have a visual record that you can refer to while speaking to the class and selecting students to contribute. It is also a good way to establish your authority and expectations; by not allowing students to choose their own seating based on friendship groups, you are clearly making a distinction between social conversation and learning. I design seating plans to be mixed gender, if possible, and I change them every half term (sooner if necessary). This encourages students to work with a wide range of different class members which can help to develop their communication skills and ideas. Initially students are disappointed that they cannot sit with their friends, but once this choice has been removed from them and it has become part of the routine in your classroom, students accept it and seem to welcome the regular change. Seating plans are also advantageous for cover teachers – they help students to keep in work mode and allow staff to identify students and follow up any behaviour issues.

I prefer students to sit in twos to minimise distractions and maximise the opportunity for paired discussion. When I want students to work in small groups, I tend to just ask them to turn their chairs around and work with the table behind them; this minimises the fuss and time spent with students selecting their own groups. If it's an extended group activity, for example a presentation to the class, I tend to let students select their own groupings but they appreciate that this is a privilege rather than the norm.

In situations where groups are going to require extra space to prepare and perform, I push all the tables to the side of the room and designate specific spaces in which students can work. Sharing a room in this way necessitates co-operation and low volume levels for it to work – it may be better to book out a large space more suited to the task, for example a drama studio. However, I would avoid the temptation to let students work outside the classroom on their own, in corridors for example. Even responsible and hard-working students have the capacity to make lots of noise that can be distracting for neighbouring classrooms. It also makes it difficult for you to keep an eye on all class members if you have to continually go outside to check other groups.

◆ Recording and collecting in homework

If you are going to take homework seriously, and expect students to as well, it is imperative that you are really organised and have systems that work. Recording homework set and making a note on the day that it is due in will help you to remember what each class is meant to be doing. This will help to avoid those awkward moments when a keen member of the class asks, 'Are you going to take our homework in then, Miss/Sir?' and your instant reaction is to ask, 'What homework?' Keeping an accurate register will also help to eliminate fake 'I wasn't here when it was set Miss/Sir' excuses.

Collecting in homework can be a time-consuming process; it can be difficult to get the lesson started due to dealing with a range of individual students and their excuses. I recommend the following strategies for managing homework:

- Ask students to do as much of their homework as possible on paper – when you ask students to present their homework on their desks it is easier to spot who has missing work. It is also easier to collect in sheets in a folder for marking rather than lumbering home a class set of exercise books and then having to trawl through them in search of the homework.
- Get students to respond with 'Yes' or 'No' when taking the register at the start of lesson according to whether they have their homework ready to hand in. This helps you to identify the students you need to speak to during the course of the lesson and allows you to record absentees that you need to chase up next lesson. In my experience, students are remarkably honest, even though some will tentatively try to get away with 'I've sort of done it'.
- If homework is on paper, rather than in books, try to collect it during a quiet moment in the lesson while students are getting on with their work; this prevents a mad rush before the bell.

- If students need to hand in their books, try to pass around a glue stick during the lesson so that you aren't greeted with an avalanche of worksheets when you open up the books at home, or even more disastrously, when a gust of wind blows the books open in the school car park.
- If you are intending to mark books at school, get students to hand them in open on a particular page, either from where you last marked it, or on the page the homework is on – this will save you time flicking through books.

Have a clear sanctions policy for students that fail to meet homework deadlines; this is only really possible if you keep an accurate record of the tasks. If students persistently fail to hand in work, make contact with parents as soon as possible to flag up the issue; I find parental involvement the most effective way of improving the standard of a students' homework – most parents are keen to support you and will appreciate being able to get involved straightaway, rather than waiting to find out in their child's report or at the next parents' evening. If the problem persists, increase sanctions and get other staff involved such as your Head of Department and the student's form tutor and Head of Year. Having some leniency is fine, but if you are seen to be a soft touch, students will start to prioritise other teachers' homework over yours. If you set up a clear policy with Year 7s and stick to it, you are less likely to have issues chasing coursework from the same individuals when they are in Year 11.

◆ Handing out and collecting in resources

If you plan to circulate a range of resources during the course of the lesson, you risk spending the first five minutes of the next lesson, or your break time, frantically trying to clear desks and collate worksheets. This can be particularly awkward if you need to vacate the room for another colleague or dash off for a duty. I recommend the following tips to try to keep resources organised in the lesson and make a sharp exit at the end:

- If you intend to use a wide range of materials in your lesson, consider creating a pack, tray or basket for each desk or group, to avoid having to hand out and collect in different materials separately.
- Secure sorting cards with oversized paperclips or clips – they are not as easy to lose or break, so it is more likely that students will be able to give whole sets of cards back in.

- Try to print reusable resources that you want students to hand back on coloured paper or card so that they are easy to spot.
- Laminate card sort activities that you want to reuse; this makes them less flimsy and more durable. Also, make sure that you make the cards large enough for students to handle easily.
- Collect used resources periodically through the lesson and get students to help you; this prevents a mad panic and a pile of mixed up resources that need sorting out at the end.

Effective classroom interaction

◆ *Making instructions and expectations explicit*

Classrooms are busy places, full of commands and information. It can be confusing for students to digest and retain a whole host of complicated instructions that were given out at the start of an activity, so try to disseminate your directions on a 'need to know' basis. When first starting out in teaching, it's comforting to start your lesson by explaining everything that students will be doing for the hour, almost running through your lesson plan. However, while it's important that students have a sense of direction and purpose, they may get overloaded with unnecessary detail. Thinking through your lesson before you walk into the classroom, or talking it through in advance with a colleague or mentor, should help to eliminate the need to do this in front of a class.

When giving important information or instructions, make sure that you have the class's full attention; it's easy to get into the habit of talking over students if you do not achieve full silence, but this will prevent all students from knowing what is expected of them. Wait for everybody's attention before speaking to the class and deal with any interruptions according to your behaviour sanctions – if visual cues and oral reminders don't work, I tend to walk over and stand next to the offending student. If the classroom is busy with discussion, again wait until you have everyone's attention before introducing an instruction.

Try to back up oral instructions by displaying them on the board as well; students can then remind themselves of what's expected without constantly needing your attention. This is also useful for students who weren't fully listening or have arrived to the lesson late. Also try to display the success criteria so that students can remind themselves of what they are expected to achieve. If a large number of students don't understand the original instruction, avoid merely repeating it in the same way – try to change your phrasing or illustrate with examples or suggestions to make your original instruction more accessible.

◆ Building up a rapport with students

One of the most important keys to good learning, motivation and behaviour is the relationships within the classroom. If teachers and pupils are antagonistic towards each other, this has a negative impact on the students' capacity for learning. Arguably, a class in which students are treated with anonymity and indifference also undermines their incentive to learn and achieve.

If you are well-prepared and confident, you can focus your attention on engaging students within the lesson. English lessons are often characterised by whole-class discussions and this is a great way to get to know the students and involve as many as possible within the lesson. Giving students 'air time' shows that you value their contributions and ideas and can help to build up a good rapport with individuals, especially if you take interest in what has been said. Creating a positive atmosphere is crucial to building a good relationship with a class.

Even more important than this is making time to speak to students individually on a one-to-one basis, rather than in front of the rest of the class. Avoid lessons dominated by up-the-front delivery; instead make time to circulate the class and speak to students about their work.

The use of humour is a common tool used by teachers to create a relaxed, familiar atmosphere. Students also appreciate teachers who don't take themselves too seriously and are capable of sharing a laugh if something funny happens. However, it is important that humour is executed sensitively; if students are not on the same wavelength, then your quips could be interpreted as sarcastic and insulting, thus undermining rather than strengthening the learning relationships within the classroom.

◆ Tips for praise and feedback – making it personal

While students and parents appreciate written praise and feedback, recognising a student's achievements as they occur with some public or personal praise can have far more impact; it's a case of spotting achievements and giving students recognition for their efforts. However, although praising students has the capacity to engage, enthuse and inspire them to do well, it loses its value if it is used indiscriminately.

Try to congratulate specific successes, rather than offering blanket praise, e.g. 'Well done for using a range of punctuation in that passage, it's made your sentences far more effective', instead of 'Well done, good work'. Students are more likely to feel worthy of the attention and proud of their accomplishments. Using students' names and showing that you have identified specific achievements and areas for development also suggests that you are interested in them as individuals.

Sharing praise with other colleagues and students' parents is also effective. Make an effort to pass on news of a student's achievements to their form tutor, Head of Year and other subject teachers; it is good for students to know that we talk about their successes instead of the things they have done wrong. Similarly, a quick phone call or postcard home is appreciated by parents and students.

◆ *Planning for a range of interactions to take place*

When planning your lessons, try to ensure that you allow for a range of interaction among students and the teacher, including whole-class, paired/group and teacher/pupil discussion. English lessons are often characterised by teacher-led discussions, but, on their own, they rarely allow all students to test out and share their ideas, and they are usually dominated by a few confident or attention-seeking individuals. I suggest embedding approaches that expect all students to participate in your lessons. The 'no-hands up' rule is one way of moving towards more varied contributions, but only if the teachers keep track of who has already contributed. One strategy is to tick names off a seating plan or assign individual numbers to pupils so that you can select individuals at random. However, this kind of approach can put students on edge, especially if they do not have an opinion or answer ready to share when they are chosen at random.

I recommend building in thinking and talking time, before engaging in whole-class discussion; this gives students the opportunity to test out their ideas and understanding without having to expose them to the rest of the class. I regularly incorporate involuntary turn-taking with class reading – all students know that they will be expected to read a paragraph during the course of the lesson so they are not surprised when their name is called out. If it is a mixed ability set, I tend to read ahead to select appropriate passages where the vocabulary is not too challenging, but once you have created a supportive learning environment, students shouldn't be embarrassed if they need help to pronounce a word. Using a Mexican-wave-style feedback during the register or a plenary is a good way of getting all students used to sharing their work with the rest of the class, however shy they are; they only have to pick one word, phrase or sentence to read out in turn. Since everyone does it quickly, this reduces potential embarrassment or a reluctance to contribute.

Freeing up sections of lesson time to walk around the class to speak to students is important, but be wary of always doing the same circuit and giving your time to the same individuals. Some students command more attention due to behavioural issues or the need for support, but avoid neglecting other members of the class at their expense. I recommend sitting down next to a few individuals per lesson and having a proper conversation about their work, in place of doing several superficial laps of the whole class every lesson just to check that students are OK.

◆ *Being approachable*

If you want to be approachable you need to allow time for students to be able to ask you questions, and not just in front of the whole class. Developing a rapport so that students are confident enough to ask for help and guidance relies on having a good learning relationship. Speaking to students outside of the classroom and about things other than the lesson content can help to demonstrate interest and develop trust. I also recommend modulating your voice so that the tone you use to speak to individuals is calmer and quieter than the one you use in front of a whole class; if your volume remains consistently loud, students may be wary of you broadcasting their conversation or query to the whole class and this may prevent them from seeking assistance in the first place.

◆ *Smile (before Christmas)*

I find the old adage 'Don't smile before Christmas' is outdated and unhelpful; it assumes that students won't behave for teachers

unless they are moody and serious, and that smiling at students reveals a chink in your classroom management armour. Some teachers successfully adopt this policy for the whole of their teaching career, not just the first term; being elusive and emotionless can seem to command respect from students but more often than not, it engenders fear. I would rather foster trust and respect with students – this is more motivating than scaring students with a detached and affected stance. While I don't advocate attempting to befriend students (it is important to have distinct boundaries and clearly-defined roles) there is nothing wrong with smiling and saying, 'Hello' as students enter the classroom, laughing at something funny, or showing that you care and take an interest in your students – this is what humans do!

◆ *Creating a positive learning environment*

Avoid dominating your lessons with negative exchanges, or constantly nagging or moaning at students. Try to have more positive than negative encounters otherwise your job satisfaction will take a knock and students will stop enjoying your lessons. Most of the time behaviour issues involve the minority; therefore avoid lecturing the entire class about expectations – find opportunities to direct this at the few who do need reminding. Kneeling down next to a disruptive child's desk and lowering your voice to whisper to give an instruction to them can be far more powerful than shouting at them from the other side of the classroom; this approach also prevents creating a negative, tense and awkward atmosphere for the rest of the class.

With examination classes, it's easy to create anxiety and switch some students off by constantly referring to the importance of grades and revision. By being more light-hearted and upbeat in your approach, students are more likely to enjoy the lessons and have their own incentive to achieve.

Making the most of lesson time

◆ *Sustaining effective pace and timings*

Keeping an appropriate sense of pace is important: it ensures that curriculum content gets covered in a productive way and keeps students engaged and motivated, this also minimises low-level disruption resulting from boredom.

When planning your lessons it's important to consider how long activities will take, to make sure that you have planned a suitable range of tasks to sustain momentum. However, making sure that there is suitable pace and challenge is reliant on reading the atmosphere in the classroom and moving things on quicker or slower than anticipated according to the progress and needs of the class.

When starting out in teaching, it's easy to let concentration and motivation dip by spending too long delivering the lesson from the front of the class; try to keep introductions, instructions and feedback snappy to avoid this. Keep your eye on the clock or make use of a timer in order to focus on the pace of the lesson – if you get carried away talking to the class or supporting students, your cue may be students yawning or putting their hand up because they've finished and have nothing else to do. Also, avoid insisting that all students complete a task before moving on to the next one – students will work at their own pace and it's unfair to make students wait for others to finish. Have extension tasks ready and be clear about what you expect students to complete, e.g. what *must*, *should* and *could* they attempt to do in the lesson?

◆ Keeping students focused and on-task

Variety and pace is crucial to keeping students engaged in the lesson. Organising lesson time into chunks breaks up the monotony of tasks and prevents students' concentration span from waning. Even if you have dedicated the majority of the lesson time to one particular task, for instance, a creative group work activity, try to create 'pit-stops' – small pauses where students can reflect, share or evaluate what they have done so far. This helps students to retain their focus; if students know that they have a large amount of time to work on a task they may lack the incentive to use their time wisely.

◆ Minimising administration

Administrative tasks such as handing out books or resources, or collecting in homework or reply slips can take up valuable chunks of lesson time. Develop ways of getting students to help out with these procedures and avoid making the whole class wait while they happen. Try to circulate materials in advance of the lesson or hand out resources or homework while the class is busily engaged in a starter activity. Also try to catch up with students during the course of the lesson while everyone else is working, rather than asking individual students to publicly explain why they haven't completed their homework in front of the whole class.

◆ Tips for useful use of registration time

Taking the register can also seem like wasted time; every lesson a minute or more can be used with students passively answering their names. Consider taking the register independent of the students by just scanning the class – if you have a seating plan it's easy to see who is missing. Alternatively make registration time useful by making it serve a second purpose. For example by asking students to:

- Respond with 'Yes' or 'No' according to whether they have their homework ready to hand in – this quickly identifies the students you need to speak to about homework during the course of the lesson.
- Share an effective word or phase that they wrote last lesson/during the starter/earlier on in the lesson (it's not always essential to take the register at the very start of the hour).
- Revise a language feature by getting students to call out an example of an adjective, persuasive device, pronoun, etc.

◆ Being flexible – improvising

Remember that your lesson plan is not a strait jacket: no one other than you knows that the task you intended to last for ten minutes has actually only taken the students 30 seconds to complete. Don't be afraid to deviate from your plan in order to achieve a more appropriate sense of pace, even if you are being observed and are anxious to stick to your plan. A colleague or inspector is more interested in the quality of learning taking place in the lesson, rather than what you planned to achieve.

Likewise, you may find it necessary to extend an aspect of your lesson, for instance the starter activity, because students find it more challenging or interesting than you had anticipated. It is better to do this than leave students confused about the topic, or stifle their enthusiasm. If you are just going through the motions, regardless of the students' level of understanding or engagement, this is not constructive or helpful. However, beware of stretching one lesson's content over several lessons on a regular basis – this might indicate that either your planning is too ambitious and doesn't suit the demands of your students, or you have a tendency to labour a point or go off on a tangent. Always prioritise lesson tasks when being flexible with content; it's not advisable to plough through a scheme of work, task by task, even though you are always overrunning, to then discover that you don't have enough time to complete the unit and therefore have to miss out important assessment tasks.

Engaging students

◆ Using a variety of teaching styles and learning activities

While teachers have their own teaching styles and preferences, it's important to remember that students learn in different ways, therefore it's important to keep your repertoire varied. Students quickly tire of monotonous lesson formats that leave little to the imagination. Fortunately, turning to the next page of a textbook every lesson is less likely in English than perhaps in other subjects, but some English teachers still resort to formulated and predictable approaches, perhaps favouring whole-class discussions, comprehension responses or long passages of reading. Reflecting on the types of learning activities that you use regularly in your lessons can help you to consciously vary them.

Despite having some credence in the concept of different learning styles, I believe that all students benefit from developing a range of approaches; limiting kinaesthetic learners to active tasks that enable them to move around the classroom, while prompting visual learners to rely on mind maps and pictures, is not only a logistical nightmare but assumes that students excel in only one method and wouldn't benefit from using other learning strategies. Planning for a range of different activities within a lesson, encompassing a variety of learning approaches, will not only help students to develop new skills and methods, it will keep them engaged and interested.

◆ Using stimulating and engaging resources

Students are media savvy and spend a lot of their spare time watching television, playing computer games and using the internet; therefore endless talk and chalk is unlikely to keep them engaged. Try to provide a range of stimulus to keep lessons lively, interesting and relevant. Short video clips, bursts of music and colourful visuals can help students to be engaged by the most mundane of subject matter. It's also important to make paper resources attractive and eye-catching; perhaps including a thought-provoking image or catchy title, this gives students more incentive to read further.

◆ Tips for making the most of interactive whiteboards

Interactive whiteboards are becoming increasingly commonplace in English classrooms, but their capacity to engage students is dependent on how they are used. Many teachers, if brave enough to switch them on, use whiteboards as little more than glorified blackboards or, at best, overhead projectors. While note making and displaying resources to the class is useful, interactive whiteboards have far more to offer. If you are lucky enough to have access to one, but don't have the skills or confidence to use it in your lessons, seek training from a colleague or INSET provider to get up to speed. It's important to get used to using one without expecting to be proficient in every respect; only with practice and familiarity will you gain experience and expertise. Furthermore, students are more patient and helpful if you encounter a technical glitch than you might expect.

By pre-preparing lesson files using accompanying software you can create extra cohesion and pace in your lessons; instead of turning your back on the class and spending several minutes writing up instructions and questions, all of this information can be typed up and ready to display. You can also present text and images in a far more inviting and eye-catching way and design activities that involve manipulation and problem solving.

It's important to remember that interactive whiteboards are just one tool at the teacher's disposal; they should complement and enhance existing, effective teaching strategies. For example, group card sort activities can be shared and discussed by moving electronic versions of the cards on the screen; students can annotate and edit scanned copies of their work in front of the class.

Although IAWB's have been developed to create the capacity for student involvement and interactivity in a lesson, if teachers dominate from the front and students are expected to watch passively, then more staring than sharing is taking place, doing little to improve traditional didactic teaching methods.

Allowing students to use the board as much as possible for manipulating objects and text will help to maximise their potential. If you have additional technology at your disposal, such as remote mice or keyboards, which are fairly cheap, you can allow students to select or move objects and edit or add text from anywhere in the classroom, increasing the level of interactivity even further. If you are lucky enough to have more expensive editions such as tablet PCs at your disposal, they can be used to project and share students' work from around the room.

◆ Choosing an appropriate teaching style – all-singing, all-dancing or low input?

Your style of delivery is also likely to alter according to the group you are teaching, the time of day or point in the term. At the start of your teaching career and when being observed, you will tend to pull out all the stops to deliver an enthusiastic performance; filled with pace, praise and, unless you are careful, the sound of your own voice. While this kind of approach may impress students and visitors, it does not necessarily lead to good learning outcomes, and if it characterises every lesson both you and your students will become exhausted.

Once settled into your teaching and confident with your classes, you may adopt a more light-touch approach; giving very little input and allowing students to get on with tasks independently. Again, this has benefits for both staff and students, but if you find yourself doing very little to support students and are instead using lesson time to catch up with e-mails or mark books, then this is clearly disadvantaging your students.

◆ Allowing your teaching style to shine through without becoming predictable

In order to enjoy your job and avoid feeling like you are delivering lessons in an emotionless, almost robotic style, it's important to let your interests and personality affect the way that you teach. Students value different teaching styles and approaches, and finding out that teachers are unique human beings that have their own passions, views and preferences. However, by sharing anecdotes, hobbies and personal reflections with students, realise that you are modelling the behaviour you expect from them so don't be surprised if lessons sometimes go off on a tangent. Also, while sharing personal interests with students can be endearing and help to forge trusting learning relationships, continually harping on about your favourite football team/band or sharing too much personal information in an attempt to win over students, can actually have the opposite effect.

Furthermore, while students benefit from having a range of different teaching styles, it is important that you don't fall into a formulaic mode of delivery. Watching colleagues and reflecting on practice will help to develop your repertoire.

Effective lesson progression and transitions

◆ *Tips for crossing the learning threshold*

It can sometimes be a challenge to get lessons going and make the best use of the first ten minutes; if students straggle in gradually and you wait for complete silence before taking the register and explaining the first task, you may end up wasting the start of a lesson. Try to have a task already displayed on the board that students can tackle as soon as they enter the room. It could be a question to answer relating to the last lesson, or stimulus to generate ideas and discussion about what is going to follow.

If you are stuck without a projector or unable to display an activity straightaway, you could circulate a task before the lesson, or at the very start, to enable students to engage with the first activity. This gives them a focus and a motivation to settle quickly, otherwise students will become restless and are likely to start off-task conversations while they are waiting for the lesson to begin.

One good strategy is to build homework tasks into the start of the lesson. A regular favourite is to ask students to swap their homework to peer evaluate – they can then be asked to share something successful that their partner has achieved during the register call. This is also a good way for you to gauge who has not done the homework.

◆ *Tips for snappy starters*

It is easy for the starter to become teacher-led instructions; try to get students active as early as possible in the lesson; they will get bored if they are expected to sit and listen for the first fifteen minutes of every lesson. Even when you have planned a task that will take most of the lesson, e.g. an essay response, try to build in some time for a starter activity that will get students engaged and thinking for themselves. Setting challenges is a good idea, for example: 'You have three minutes to think of five persuasive devices that we studied last lesson', or 'Five minutes to draw a pen-portrait of Miss Haversham and label with at least five facts about her character'. This will inject pace into the lesson, and the use of specific success criteria helps students to realise how much they are expected to achieve in the given time frame. It also helps students to make connections with prior learning.

Tests and quizzes can also be a good way to get students motivated and on task. Tried and tested favourites such as Blockbusters and True or False can generate a good sense of competition. A good strategy is to include some questions that they don't yet know the answers to, but will do by the end of the lesson. This helps to create cohesion and relevance between the different parts of the lesson.

◆ *Tips for effective plenary activities*

Plenaries tend to be even more neglected than starters, often because every other aspect of the lesson overruns, leaving frantic packing away and scribbling down homework as the only signal that it is the end of the lesson. Plenary activities help students to consolidate what they have learnt in the lesson, so it is important to make time for them. The easiest plenary activity is to ask students to return to the lesson objectives and evaluate their success, either through a question/answer format or by getting them into the habit of writing reflective learning journals. I find this particularly useful for lessons in which little written work has been achieved, for example a speaking and listening lesson. Another tried and tested technique is to build in time for self/ peer evaluation of the work that has been produced in the lesson.

While all of these strategies can prove useful, try to vary plenary tasks to avoid them becoming staid and meaningless. A whizzy end to the lesson with an interactive quiz can create a memorable ending. You could also provide a taster of what is to come in the next lesson. If you put the effort into an interesting activity, you are more likely to make the time for it to happen.

◆ Smooth transition between activities

It is really important to plan for a clear sequence of learning activities so that students are able make connections between the different tasks that they are being asked to complete. In your mind, the links may be obvious, but it's important to make them explicit to students by the way in which your lesson is delivered.

Clear explanation of transitions is important. Including the outline of the lesson and how individual activities fit in with the big picture is also a good idea. Make sure that you have the students' full attention if you are introducing new instructions – it is tempting to talk over the bustle of a busy classroom, especially if students are involved in on-task discussion, but otherwise you are ultimately going to end up explaining the task separately to thirty individuals. If it is not essential to stop the class to get their attention, you can use other means to explain transition, perhaps flashing new instructions on the board or circulating a task sheet for students to move on to when they are ready.

Having a pre-prepared sequence of slides to accompany each stage of the lesson is a great tool. Software such as Smart Notebook can enable you to create a complete file including all of the instructions and task descriptions needed for the lesson. You can then also attach associated resources and hyperlinks to create smooth transitions at the tip of your fingers.

Promoting active learning

◆ Sharing objectives with students and encouraging them to reflect on their learning

Most teachers recognise the importance of clear objectives being communicated to students; many display them prominently on their boards at the start of every lesson. However, merely flashing curriculum speak at students may do little to actively engage them with the lesson's goals and rationale. A lot of the time, what teachers actually end up communicating to the students is, 'What we are going to do today is. . .' rather than the learning intentions.

It is important to use student-friendly language to explain the learning objectives and to keep focused on the skills and knowledge that students will develop, rather than the activities that they are expected to complete. As well as introducing objectives at the start of the lesson, it's important to revisit them throughout to keep you and the students focused on the intended learning outcomes.

One successful strategy that I use within schemes of work is rephrasing the learning objective statements into questions. For example, modifying the composition objective 2.3n from the English Programme of Study: 'Pupils should be able to use persuasive techniques and rhetorical devices' to 'Can you use persuasive techniques and rhetorical devices?' I also try to add an element of evaluation to the phrasing of these learning objective questions such as 'How effectively can you...?' If you then develop the practice of returning to objectives in the plenary, the question format prompts students to judge their level of success. You can also differentiate the objectives by providing a range of answers from which students can select the most appropriate response, for example, 'I have used a range of persuasive devices to a sophisticated effect'; 'I have used rhetorical questions and repetition to some effect' or 'I have tried to use rhetorical questions for effect'.

Promoting thinking and independent learning

◆ Effective questioning

English teachers rely heavily on questioning in their lessons, and yet very little time is spent planning the phrasing, type and style of questions, and considering how they should be used within the lesson. Simple closed questions are often used in starter activities to trigger students' prior learning and 'warm up' a class. Easy questions may be good to build students confidence and remind them what they know, but if they aren't demanding enough to help students to develop their learning or understanding, then there is not much point to them. Try to promote high-order thinking by posing open, challenging questions that involve more cognitive processing by requiring students to synthesise, analyse and evaluate information instead of merely recalling it.

Planning good questions will help to develop the quality of the problem solving that you ask students to engage in; if you rely on improvising questions during the course of your lesson, there will be a tendency to stick to questions that test knowledge and understanding.

Also try to present your questions in a variety of ways; English teachers tend to rely on two questioning formats, either oral discussion or written comprehension. The two tend to complement each other – time to discuss questions before writing them down and also completing reading comprehension and then comparing responses. Try to vary the interplay of written and oral responses and also endeavour to display your questions clearly rather than just saying them – students benefit from being able to refer back to questions, rather than having to remember what you said.

◆ Thinking time

The average wait time that a teacher allows before asking for a response to their question is between three and five seconds. While this quick-fire approach may help to develop a sense of pace, it can impede the quality of students' responses and limit the number of students who are prepared to contribute. Such keenness to elicit answers also implies that teachers' expect students to know an answer straightaway, therefore suggesting that the questions aren't as challenging or useful as they could be. Giving students the chance to consider what you have asked and formulate a response will hopefully lead to more reflective and developed answers – it should also mean that you can ask any member of the class to contribute without entirely putting them on the spot. I'd also recommend building in some talk time after you have introduced some questions; this enables students to test out and share their ideas in small groups before volunteering them to the rest of the class.

◆ Removing structures and scaffolds

Students benefit from frameworks and prompts to support their work, especially with challenging tasks. Plan for gradual removal of such support mechanisms so that students aren't eternally dependent on teacher direction, incapable of thinking, writing or speaking for themselves. If students stick to prescriptive essay plans and formulaic approaches they are likely to flounder when they encounter an unexpected style of task. A key problem with exam groups is that many are reliant on spoon-feeding; building up students' confidence and stamina will help them to achieve independently.

◆ *Revision lessons – avoiding death by practice papers*

Paradoxically, although revision is supposed to optimise independent learning, many English students in the lead up to exams become more passive and reliant on teachers than they have ever been. It's important that you help students to develop a tool kit of skills with which to approach a range of exam tasks with increasing confidence. Many GCSE candidates treat us as all-knowing oracles, desperate to know the right way of doing things and the right answer. It may be tempting to endlessly spoon-feed and practise model answers to exam papers; this does little to promote students' independent application of skills and knowledge – try to plan for an approach that allows for increasing autonomy.

Many students believe, misguidedly, that it's impossible to revise for English exams. It is important that students realise that English revision is based more on developing skills than recalling information; while reading cue cards containing a wealth of facts, dates and formulas may be invaluable for other subjects, students will benefit little from merely revising the content of examination texts and a glossary of literary terms. Revision guides do little to promote active revision strategies; resources are often crammed full of text seemingly based on the assumption that merely reading top tips about the process of writing an essay or completing a comprehension response will somehow improve the students' own ability to do this. Try to provide students with a range of revision materials and activities that will enable them to practise their own skills, not just theorise about them.

Practice responses are vital in developing students' exam practice, but like any other teaching strategy, using past papers should be done sparingly to avoid overkill. Students should be encouraged to look at past papers and mark schemes to become familiar with format and requirements, but it is not necessary to expect them to answer the whole paper – cherry pick aspects of the materials that students will engage with and benefit from. If you have a class that is brilliant at writing descriptions, try to target their focus on the other writing triplets or the reading aspect of the same paper, rather than indiscriminately setting up a double lesson for them to complete the entire paper. While it's beneficial to spend some time planning and discussing how to approach a response together, students also need to be given the experience of tackling this kind of task independently, before they do it for real in the exam hall. On the flip side of this, it is pointless setting endless practice papers for students to complete in silence if they are not learning from it and improving in the process. Develop a range of assessment for learning strategies to enable students to reflect on the experience and gain from it.

Also be aware of the monotony that comes with endless practice papers. It is important that students are motivated and engaged in the lead up to their exams, not bored senseless by uninspiring and formulaic revision tasks. Remember that the same skills can be practised and developed through more exciting means that a past paper – why not get students to practise their persuasive skills by focusing on a topical debate or a recent school policy change rather than the tired 'letter to your Head Teacher arguing for or against school uniform' task. Analyse the front page of a recent glossy magazine instead of a poor quality photocopy of a resource from a past paper. Basically, try to keep learning interesting. Examination classes need stimulating and motivating just as much as Year 7s, so inject some fun into your lessons to avoid students from switching off; even A level students appreciate the odd quiz!

Developing outstanding assessment practices in English

4

Principles for effective assessment

◆ *The difference between marking and assessment*

Marking can easily become the bane of English teachers' existence. In order to keep a realistic, manageable mark load, and to make sure that your time is being put to productive use, it's important to differentiate between marking and assessment. A lot of time can be spent ticking and writing comments that do little to support students' learning. Creating copious reminders to 'underline the title' and 'check spelling' is a waste of your time if the student didn't respond after the first time you wrote it. Written comments aren't always the best means to communicate suggestions or advice to students – spoken feedback can be far more powerful, plus it gives students the chance to ask further questions and get more specific and detailed suggestions.

◆ *Different types of marking – making it fit for purpose*

Your style of marking should vary according to the intended audience and purpose: marking a poem written by a shy, severely dyslexic child will differ greatly from the feedback given to an A Level student on a practice exam response, or the type of annotations that you will use on a coursework essay being sent to a GCSE moderator. It sounds obvious, but it can be easy to slip into a formulaic way of marking, e.g. circling every spelling mistake, even when it is not appropriate for the context. If the target for a given piece of work is to explain language effects on

55

the reader, make this the focus for your assessment. Although it's tempting to give feedback about grammar, sentence structure and paragraphing, if these features aren't included in the assessment criteria then you will be bombarding the student with too many aspects for improvement, possibly irrelevant ones as well. If you are marking exercise books to see how students are getting on, try to keep comments light-touch and positive. Moaning at students via a page long diatribe is unlikely to be effective. The classic 'see me next lesson' rarely prompts the student to do so, instead make a record of who you want to catch up with and have that conversation in person.

◆ Assessment for learning – making all assessment formative

Most of the time we set assessed pieces to gauge students' ability and progress. However, the most important outcome of a story, essay or comprehension task is not the mark that it gets but what students have learnt in the process, and what they do next time to create an even stronger response. As Black and Williams demonstrated in their influential paper, 'Inside the Black Box', students have been conditioned to prioritise the mark awarded at the expense of ignoring accompanying feedback. This can be very frustrating for teachers who have spent a great deal of time and effort creating purposeful, personal comments and specific targets. If you want students to focus on the formative comment, ensure that some of your assessments are comment only and in the case of pieces that are graded, students are given ample time to engage with the feedback. Yes, the first thing that students will want to do is check and compare marks with their peers, but then build in lesson time for them to read the comments and respond to them, either by way of self reflection or, even better, by giving them an opportunity to put the targets into practice straightaway; for instance, by redrafting a paragraph including the suggested improvements.

◆ Prioritising assessment – having an effective policy

New English teachers can often fall into the trap of writing more in response to a student's piece of work than the student did themselves. If you are spending an inordinate amount of time marking exercise books with little gain, then consider rethinking your approach to marking. Remember that students will benefit from choice, concise comments that will help them to see what they have done well and identify scope for improvement. Refer to departmental policy to make sure that you are in line with the school's and parents' expectations in terms of the frequency and quantity of marking. However, ultimately you've got to use your professional judgement and common sense to decide when and how to mark to best benefit your students and your sanity.

Organising and planning assessment opportunities

◆ Planning a range of assessment styles

There are a range of assessment methods to choose from, so select one appropriate to the purpose of your marking, and the amount of time that you have to commit to it. It's no good writing reams of rigorous and detailed comments if you only manage to mark four books an hour, resorting to continually handing back unmarked books because you were too exhausted to complete the set. Here is a range of possible approaches:

- *Tick and flick: glancing at books and ticking pages at random*
  This technique only serves to indicate that you have looked at students' work. Teachers can resort to this when they are behind with their marking and anxious to superficially prove to students, parents or their Head of Department that they have marked the books. It may be appropriate when checking note-taking and quality of presentation, but it does not constitute assessment and will not help students to improve.
- *Give a summative mark/level: giving a level, grade or number at the end of a piece of work*
  Some English teachers tend to adopt this approach when marking test responses or coursework. By only providing a number or letter you are not giving students any idea of how they achieved the mark or what they need to do to improve further. Other than spelling tests, which I'd recommend students marking themselves, I would always recommend at least a brief summative comment and one target.
- *Give a summative comment: a comment at the end identifying what students have achieved*

This helps students to see what you think of the work, but avoid overly generic, empty comments such as 'good work'. Also remember to use language that students will understand and give them time to read and interpret your comment, especially if it accompanies a grade.

- *Highlight errors: underline, circle or highlight grammatical mistakes*
  Most English teachers can't resist drawing attention to omitted apostrophes or mis-spelt words. It may be useful to highlight these sorts of mistakes so that students can identify common errors for revision. However, make sure that you don't get carried away with pointing out every single mistake – this can be demoralising. Also make sure that you are not prioritising this kind of mistake-spotting over more helpful guidance, especially with reading responses.

- *Annotate with literacy symbols: use a common code to indicate how students could improve*
  Using short-hand such as 'sp' for spelling error, '//' for new paragraph needed, 'cap' for capital letter and 'p' for missing punctuation, can help to identify specific errors and save time. It's important that students and parents are familiar with these symbols and, again, they are used sparingly for effect.

- *Annotate with comments: provide commentary in the margins*
  This helps to indicate specific achievements or prompts during the course of a student's piece of work. This approach is most appropriate for practice pieces or work that are going to be redrafted; it gives students the detail that they need to make improvements. This is a time-consuming practice so it's best to do for key pieces, rather than all of the time.

- *Add suggestions: provide students with prompts or questions to develop their work*
  Actually correcting students' work or adding extra phrases does little to empower students. Not only does it render them passive, it means that you are writing their work for them which has serious implications for coursework. Always try to make suggestions or ask questions that will allow students to come up with their own changes or additions.

- *Set targets for improvement: add two or three actions for improvement*
  Giving students direct and specific instructions for further improvement is a very direct, helpful assessment method. Again remember to stick to a couple of key targets rather than bombarding students with too many. Also, plan opportunities for students to put these targets in practice with a similar task in the near future.

- *Peer assessment: get students to assess each other's work*
  This is a tried and tested way to get students to share their work and judge each other's strengths and weaknesses. Make sure that you model the process first and set up expected etiquette, for instance, the 'two kisses and a wish' approach (getting students to identify two good features and one suggestion for improvement).
- *Self assessment: get students to assess their own work*
  Another way of getting students actively involved in the assessment of their own work. It is also a good way to familiarise students with success criteria. However, while this approach is also a good way to save marking time, it shouldn't be used as a cop-out when students would really benefit from a teacher's expertise and guidance.

◆ *Choosing appropriate times to assess students*

Typically, assessments usually come at the end of a scheme to judge how much students have learnt and achieved within a particular topic. However, this is not always the best time to assess students' progress. One very practical issue is that your marking will become unmanageable if every class's work is handed in at the same time, usually just before a school holiday. Also, if you leave it until the end of a unit of work to assess students' understanding, it doesn't give you any scope for putting the findings of the class assessment into action by revisiting particular skills or features before moving on to a new topic. Sometimes it's also beneficial to assess students right at the start of a scheme of work; this provides a diagnostic tool to identify students' prior knowledge. Consult departmental plans and tweak timings accordingly to make sure assessments are staggered to advantage you and your students.

◆ *Building in time to prepare students for assessment tasks*

Sometimes it is wholly appropriate to surprise students with an assessment task. However, most of the time it is best to prepare students so that they have the chance to achieve their best. The first time students attempt a difficult task, like a poetry comparison essay, it's important to model the process by breaking down the question, planning the response together, and even starting students off. Although this may inflate the marks that students get for this task, it will help to build the confidence and skills that students will need to succeed independently the next time they embark on such a task. At the very least, recap success criteria before students start an assessment.

Making marking manageable and useful

◆ Tips for levelling and annotating students' work

At the start of a scheme of work, have a clear idea of which key pieces you intend to level and annotate in detail. When marking these, select the most appropriate strategy from the suggested approaches and apply this method consistently across the class. It's easy to start off a class set of assessment with enthusiasm, annotating everything, and then by the time you get to the last piece of work you are writing the bare minimum. If a set of marking warrants detailed feedback, try to break up marking sessions to make the task more manageable. Also make sure that the way in which you level work is the same across the class, e.g. thirds of levels (5a, 4c, 7b), GCSE grades or specific marks; students will get confused and anxious if their neighbour has an 'A' grade while they have the same mark and have only been given a 'B+'.

◆ Strategies for giving meaningful feedback

Always keep in mind how your feedback will be interpreted – this will help you to stick to language that students will be able to understand and apply. It is best if feedback links to students' personal targets and directly refers to the marking criteria. However, avoid copying out lengthy and verbose phrases from the mark scheme – this may merely serve to confuse students and put them off of reading your comments.

◆ Building in opportunities for students to reflect on their feedback and ask questions

After spending hours assessing students' work, it's common for teachers to give out books at the start of the lesson and then hastily move on to new subject content. More conscientious students may strive to speed-read your comments, or read them closely at home, but in reality students will merely flick through to spot any grades or merits before focusing on the new lesson content. If you want students to engage with your feedback and make sense if it, you need to provide time in which they can do this. Assigning a few minutes and perhaps setting a question that requires them to respond to your comments, allows students to make use of the time that you have spent giving personalised written feedback.

◆ *Plan for opportunities for students to act on their targets*

Some of the best starter activities involve giving students a chance to act on their feedback immediately. For example, if you have just handed back a piece of descriptive writing, give the class ten minutes to select one paragraph for redrafting. Students will be able to act on their own specific targets, be it using a range of sentence structures for effect, adding imagery or developing more detailed description. This time dedicated to improving work shows students the importance of crafting their work, as you are asking them to hone specific details rather than rewrite the whole response. This also gives you the opportunity to circle the class and check that students understand their targets and how to apply them.

Target setting

◆ *Using diagnostic assessment*

Tick sheets can help to identify how students have achieved against specific assessment criteria. When observing a group speaking and listening performance, it can be a lot easier for you to tick the appropriate box on a pre-prepared assessment sheet including the mark scheme, rather than trying to frantically write notes about all of the individual performances. Such formats provide a visual representation of how students have performed against the criteria – it's easy for them to see, for instance, that they scored highly for engaging their audience with interesting expression and content, but did less well with Standard English appropriate for the task.

◆ *Making targets SMARTer*

Avoid over-generalised targets that students will struggle to put into action. Identifying three mis-spelt words for students to learn is far more useful than a blanket statement such as 'focus on accuracy'. Also try to give students a range of specific strategies to improve their responses. For example, if you want them to explain quotes in more detail, provide them with a range of possible aspects to explain: how the language/structure affects the reader, the author's intentions, how it links to other aspects of the book. This will give students the practical capacity to apply your targets.

◆ *Personalising target setting*

Try to be specific in your comments to show the students that you have read their work carefully; blanket praise such as 'very good' doesn't indicate that you have paid much attention to their writing and isn't very constructive. Using students' names in your feedback can also help to add a personal touch. Keeping an effective record of students' targets as well as their marks can help you to build up a picture of students' areas for development. This will help you to see progression, or spot whether you are always setting students' the same targets which they are failing to successfully meet.

Involving students with assessment

◆ *Strategies for self and peer assessment*

Including self and peer assessment opportunities in your lesson can help to empower students by making them more active, judicious and discriminatory about their work. Try to keep students positive and constructive in their comments. One particularly effective strategy is to get students to highlight the most effective phrase in a passage of writing. Students also enjoy the responsibility of using a red pen to write a summative comment, or deciding whether their peers deserve a merit. Try to give students specific assessment foci to base their judgements on.

◆ Sharing assessment criteria with students

At the heart of any Assessment for Learning (AfL) approach should be students who understand how and why they are being assessed. A common approach is to develop student-friendly descriptors and exhibit them prominently in English classrooms. However, it's unrealistic to expect students to read and internalise static display material. Try to refer to assessment criteria regularly to familiarise students with expectations; it shouldn't be something that is introduced just before the students' first external examinations.

◆ In-class assessment and AfL strategies

Rather than waiting to take books in to assess students' knowledge and skills, try to build in opportunities within lessons to do this. AfL techniques such as 'give me five' can help to gauge students' confidence with a particular topic (students hold up all five fingers to denote confidence and fewer to show how much they understand). Traffic light colours can also be used by students to indicate this. Using strategies like this halfway through a lesson can also help you to ascertain whether the class are ready to move on.

Involving parents with assessment

◆ Report writing

Good practice that relates to marking is also equally applicable to report writing. Most formats have a very restricted word count, and since subject reports are usually produced annually, it's important that you are concise and specific. Parents need to be able to understand the terminology you have used, but you also need to provide details that will help them to support their children with their English. While you may be tempted to write at length about an individual's effort and behaviour (or lack of it), keep focused on subject-specific skills. If you have got grave concerns about a student's progress, then contact home as soon as possible; don't wait for a formal reporting stage.

Using statement banks can be a good way of saving time, but avoid over-using stock phrases – this undermines and depersonalises the reporting process, especially when peers realise that they have almost identical comments. Consult departmental policy for the 'house style'. For instance, some schools use a very formal tone in the third person using student's full names, whereas other institutions may expect you to address reports to the students and abbreviations may be acceptable. Careful proof-reading is essential, even if there is another layer of checking. As an English teacher, you will be expected to set a good example. It will be both time-consuming and embarrassing if colleagues have to get back to you with report corrections.

◆ Tips for parents' evenings

Your first parents' evening can be a daunting experience – the key is to feel prepared and confident. I would recommend having a simple sheet of class information in front of you that you can refer to easily. For example, your mark book containing recent assessment marks, a record of homework and a note of any issues that you want to raise; in the fray of a busy hall, it's easy to forget these details.

Parents' evening appointments are only long enough to give a brief snapshot of a student's performance and achievements. Usually parents are running to a tight schedule so make sure that you stick to your appointments otherwise you will cause queues and delays, this will lose favour with parents as well as your colleagues.

As with report writing, try to start with something positive; refer to specific achievements and communicate direct targets for improvement. In some schools students are expected to attend with their parents; be prepared to address both parents and students and make sure that both understand what you are saying. Be warned: while some parents slip into the defensive, others may try to get you to gang up on their child. Remember to stay professional and avoid any potential conflict by making contact with parents before the evening itself if you have acute concerns about a pupil. If issues arise on the evening, make sure that you know who you can refer queries to – usually your Head of Department.

Some teachers like having a file of books or folders to refer to during the course of the appointments, but in reality you don't want to waste precious minutes leafing through paperwork trying to find work. It may be useful to pick up specific pieces for some students in order to exemplify a particular achievement or concern, but try to keep your desk uncluttered. I usually take my laptop so that I can access a range of data, but if you do this make sure that you have a power supply so it doesn't cut out halfway through the evening. It may be useful to have certain references to hand such as a recommended reading list or a letter for a potential trip – often these sorts of things get lost in students' bags and never make it home.

Recording assessment outcomes

◆ *Creating records of students' progress that they can engage with*

In many English departments, teachers create portfolios of students' work by collating key assignments as a record of students' achievements and progress. The concept of 'best work' is a good one if students are encouraged to take pride in their work and refer back to their folder of work for successes and targets for development. However, it's important not to let administration and 'copying out in neat' take over this process; the filing and organisation of the students' outcomes can become more important than the actual learning. While this is good practice for coursework, the act of presenting work well, having it assessed in detail and then storing it in the depths of a filing cabinet, only to be retrieved at the end of the year to be given back to the students to take home, may be limited in value. If your department does follow this practice, try to minimise the amount of lesson time dedicated to sorting out folders. Also incorporate ways for students to capture the feedback that you have given them – perhaps through a target sheet that they fill in when they receive assignments and review periodically.

I would advocate an 'all work is best work' approach. While it's important that key pieces are identified for assessment, if students believe that their exercise book is merely a rough jotter and that anything of worth goes into a folder in a filing cabinet, then they are not likely to put as much effort and attention into the regular written work that they produce in their books. Unless students' work is used for display purposes, I prefer them to keep all of their learning outcomes in their exercise book for reference. It's important that parents can see a record of students' accomplishments, and that students can look back to the last time they produced a similar response to identify how they can improve it.

◆ Keeping a systematic record of attainment data

It is important to have a user-friendly system that will let you keep track of students' grades. Most teachers keep a paper mark book but, from experience, they can get very crammed and messy if you wish to change marks. I would recommend storing marks on an electronic mark book using Excel. This allows you to easily change marks and add extra columns and rows. Also, rather than throwing away your mark book at the end of the year, class data can be passed on to new teachers.

I would recommend having your mark book open while you are assessing a piece of work; this enables you to input marks straightaway, rather than having to do this separately. If you are marking in a hurry you may give students their work back before having a chance to make a record of it and it will become time-consuming if you then have to catch up with each student to note down their marks retrospectively.

◆ Using your mark book to record students' targets as well as their grades

While we acknowledge that the most important aspect of the assessment process are the formative comments, not the grades, when you look at most teachers' mark books, all you can see is a set of numbers and letters. Even though teachers spend a great deal of time writing targets, few actually make a record of these. Unless you have a fantastic memory and are able to internalise and recall the skills and areas for development for all of the individuals that you teach, I would advise using a simple short-hand code to note down students' targets as well as their grades. In my electronic mark book I have an extra column for this after each grade so that I can write notes such as 'range sent, sp' (use a range of sentence structures and learn key spellings); 'det, author' (develop in detail and consider author's intentions) or 'proj, lead' (project your voice more and take a leading role'. I can refer to these targets when I set up the next assessment; they are also very useful prompts for report writing and parents' evenings.

◆ *Using assessment to track students' progress*

If you keep a regular, systematic record of students' marks, it is easy to see whether they have made sufficient progress across an academic year. When you have entered a set of data, take a little time to look back at the last piece of work that they did to compare the marks, and if you have made a note of them, the targets.

I find it useful to record marks according to type of activity rather than in chronological order. For example, I input all speaking and listening marks together, all reading marks together and all writing marks together. Students often excel in one aspect of English while struggling with another. If your marking mixes up different types of assessment tasks in order of the date on which they were marked, this can give a deceiving picture of progress. For instance, a student may have achieved a 5a for a comprehension task, a 6b for a written argument and then a 7c for a speaking and listening presentation and a 6c for a reading response essay. This sequence of marks, without accompanying details of the tasks, can make it look as though the student made fantastic progress and then slumped, but if these assessments were recorded according to type you would see that reading is their weakest area but they seem to be making some progress.

If you do keep your mark book electronically, it is easy to colour code students' data according to the level of progress they are making, either manually or by using conditional formatting. This can be a powerful visual aid, especially with exam classes, to indicate how students are performing against their predictors. I tend to use red to denote severe under-achievement, orange to show they are a grade below what they are expected to achieve, yellow to show them in line with their targets and green if they are achieving a grade above. This can help you to differentiate students according to relative performance. By hiding other rows, you can also show this to students and parents to discuss an individual's progress. With coursework grades, for instance, the use of colour is a helpful way of highlighting which pieces they would benefit from redrafting.

◆ *Using data to inform planning*

Another benefit of having a systematic record of a class's data is that it helps you to spot patterns of strength or weakness across a cohort. If you notice that the whole class under-performed on an extract-based essay task, then it helps you to realise that they will need more support and time spent on the skills necessary for this type of task. It may also get you to reflect on how you prepared the students for the essay. Perhaps next time you should go about it in a different way if the vast majority of the class did not seem to perform very well. The benefit of making a note of students' individual targets, as well as their marks, is that this helps to identify very specific areas for development where students would benefit from extra support or practice.

Tool kit for teaching Speaking and Listening

5

Principles for effective speaking and listening

◆ The power of speech

The ability to communicate effectively is a key skill that English teachers have the responsibility to develop. Confident speech and perceptive listening will not only help students to achieve in English and across other subjects, it will also give them an advantage in all aspects of their future; it is therefore important that you plan for this to happen.

◆ Speaking and listening to support reading, writing and thinking in the English classroom

Students benefit from being able to talk through their work with others. Providing time for students to speak about a text or written task helps them to generate, select and develop their ideas. Many students also learn from talk – discussing a concept can help them to create new links and understanding. Therefore, the way in which you structure students' talk with prompts and questions can affect how well they engage with an English topic or task.

◆ Giving speaking and listening adequate status and time

Although talk happens all the time in English classrooms, learning discreet speaking and listening skills is rarely given as much focus and attention as other aspects of the syllabus. Coined as the 'Cinderella' of English teaching, speaking and listening only tends to come to the fore in Key Stage 4 classes where it starts to count towards a GCSE grade. However, even then, it tends to be side-lined to a few lessons where students get very little time to prepare and develop their skills, whereas whole weeks are dedicated to written coursework that is worth the same or less than one speaking and listening assignment.

When planning schemes of work, try to ensure that speaking and listening tasks are given as much kudos as written responses. Also, include opportunities for students to learn and practise new skills, rather than merely expecting students to perform, as though it were some innate and fixed ability that does not need improvement.

◆ Assessing and developing speaking and listening skills

Like any other assessment, speaking and listening tasks merit good assessment for learning practices. If students are going to improve their skills in this area, they need to have good modelling, preparation and feedback. While classroom discussion happens all of the time, you need to build in regular opportunities for students to develop their speaking and listening skills in formal and informal contexts.

◆ Organising talk time

Avoid a few students from dominating classroom talk by using a range of strategies to involve all class members as much as possible:

- Build in time for paired and group discussion:
  Shy students may not wish to share their ideas and understanding publicly in front of the whole class, but will be able to do this more confidently in small groups.
- No-hands-up:
  English teachers usually rely on asking students who volunteer their responses; by implementing a 'no-hands-up' approach, the expectation is that any students could be asked to contribute at any time. While this may serve to keep students on their toes, it can also prove quite daunting for students if they don't feel ready to share their ideas. If you do use this method, make sure that you give students a chance to think about the answers and talk about it with others before sharing with the whole class.

- Talk tokens:
  If you have a group in which only a small number of students dominate classroom talk, try to use strategies to provide more equity, otherwise this will only serve to make proficient speakers even more confident and could make reluctant speakers even more reluctant to get involved. Try introducing talk tokens, the idea being that everyone has two slips of paper to use during a debate, for instance. This prevents the chattier individuals making all the contributions and prompts the others to get involved.

◆ *Developing students' skills and confidence*

One issue that some Key Stage 4 English teachers face is a student who refuses to talk in front of the class, making it impossible for them to assess them for GCSE purposes. In order to avoid this awkward stand-off, it's important to incorporate the practice of speaking and listening from Year 7 onwards. Building up students' stamina with small, informal tasks will help to make public speaking less threatening.

To start with, you may wish to assess students as you walk around the class, rather than expecting them to stand at the front. Remember that students are more likely to engage with a task if it's engaging and fun, try to choose activities that students will want to partake in, rather than argue against.

If students really struggle with speaking in front of others, for genuine reasons, recreate an audience at lunch time by getting them to bring along their friends to watch. This makes sure that you are fulfilling exam requirements in a situation where students feel confident. You might also find that students lose their inhibitions when they realise that they are going to have to give up their own time.

Capitalising on talk in the classroom

◆ *Building in talk time to develop thinking*

As mentioned previously, talk can be a powerful tool for students to develop their understanding and thinking. Bear this in mind before expecting students to answer questions immediately or asking them to carry out tasks independently and in complete silence. Incorporate chunks of lesson time that allow students to talk about their ideas, and appreciate that a chatty classroom isn't always a bad thing; if it's on-task talk, then students are likely to be learning from the experience rather than wasting time, as you might fear.

◆ Planning a range of contexts and opportunities for speech

Speaking and listening assessments shouldn't always involve presenting a speech in front of the class. As GCSE requirements expect students to exhibit a range of speaking and listening skills in a variety of contexts, students need to develop experience of this throughout Key Stage 3 and beyond. Over the course of a year, aside from the regular classroom discussion that takes place, students should have a chance to exhibit their speaking and listening skills and receive formative assessment. I recommend one task per scheme of work that enables them to do this, varying between individual, group and drama-based activities for a range of different purposes.

◆ Promoting and developing listening skills

Often teachers and students alike assume that good listening skills are tantamount to students being silent while others perform. Like any other English skill, listening should be explicitly taught and assessed and students should be given a range of strategies to develop their competencies. Focusing on the following may help students to appreciate how they can demonstrate good listening skills:

- Non-verbal cues such as nodding to show agreement with the speaker.
- Responding to a point that the speaker has made.
- Building upon a point made by someone else.
- Probing speakers further by improvising appropriate questions.
- Challenging points raised by other people.

Individual presentations

◆ Giving students scope and independence

If students are expected to sustain a talk for a number of minutes on a particular topic, it is important that you give them the chance to talk about something that is important or meaningful to them. Sometimes it may be appropriate to give students complete free rein to choose their subject matter, but usually it's best to supply them with a range of possible ideas to prevent them from floundering or panicking about the task.

Open-ended tasks such as talking about a particular moment or object that is significant to them can create very powerful and personal talks. Likewise, allowing students to research and present to the class a topic that they feel strongly about can also allow you to get a flavour of students' personalities and interests. However, be sensitive to the fact that some students may feel uncomfortable divulging personal information – it's important that the classroom feels like a trusting and safe environment and students have the option of presenting more impersonal subject matters.

The staple individual presentation involves students reporting back on their work experience. This tends to work well at the end of Year 10 when students are curious to find out about each other's placements, and they have lots of experiences that they can share. However, it's important that students are properly briefed and prepared so that the presentations are lively and entertaining, rather than dull and monotonous.

◆ *Helping students to prepare and deliver their presentations*

The amount of support that students need to prepare a successful speech will depend on their skills and confidence. I would recommend providing a loose framework and making this optional for higher ability students. With weaker or less confident individuals, I would provide more detailed plans and opening sentences that will help them to structure their content. Be careful not to be too prescriptive though; students can end up feeling as though there is a 'right' approach or sequence. Promote improvisation and minimal notes where possible to allow students to achieve a higher mark.

◆ *Making presentations professional and meaningful*

It is important that students feel as though they are speaking for a real audience and purpose, even if it's part of a lesson among their peers. Clear, commonly-agreed ground rules based on mutual respect should enable students to have the class's full attention. Also, agree whether questions and feedback are expected during

the presentation or should wait until the end. Creating an appropriate setting can help to give the talk the appropriate focus. Having relevant backdrops or props, such as a lectern, can help with this, as can moving the classroom furniture to make it more conducive to listening to a presentation.

Students may wish to accompany their presentation with PowerPoint to make it more professional, but make students aware of the pitfalls, otherwise using ICT can actually hinder rather than help them. Some advice for successful use of accompanying slides is:

- Keep text minimal.
- Only have key words on your slides, not full sentences.
- Never read out the content on your slides (this shouldn't be possible if they have only used key words).
- Try to use images, rather than text, as an *aide-memoire*.
- Make sure that slide content is large and clearly visible to all in the room.
- Avoid an excessive number of transitions that you need to click through on each slide.
- Look at your audience, not the screen.
- Avoid annoying transition sequences and noises that will distract your audience and take the attention away from the content of your speech.

Group activities

◆ *Selecting relevant topics*

The best kinds of topics will be those that promote debate and prompt students to argue with each other straightaway. Tried-and-tested issues such as fox-hunting, euthanasia and smoking in public places are favourites of English teachers, but beware of choosing out-of-date topics or ones that students may be indifferent towards. It may be best to choose something topical or contextually linked to a text that you have been studying. Some examples could be a debate on the influence of nature versus nurture in regards to whether Frankenstein is born a monster or becomes one as a result of maltreatment; a group review of a film adaptation of a Shakespeare play they have studied; a council meeting debating the abolition of Christmas day as mooted by Ebenezer Scrooge.

◆ *Assigning specific roles and groupings*

One of the key ingredients to a successful group activity is individual members having clearly-defined roles. This may involve prescribing responsibilities such as chair, secretary, etc., in advance but, most importantly, the allocation of roles should ensure that everyone has the chance to make a significant contribution to the task and develop and demonstrate their skills – giving someone the role of silent note-taker is clearly going to disadvantage them.

I find that giving students a particular character role can help them to develop language and ideas appropriate to the task – it also makes sure that there are enough contradicting views and positions to develop and sustain debate within the performance. For example, for the film review task, I turn this into a Radio 4 culture programme in which one student is the presenter, interviewing the guests, another is the film director and then the two remaining roles are an English teacher and a GCSE student. This gives the task more of a context to work with, rather than students feeling as though they are merely having an informal chat about their own views.

◆ *Developing students' debating skills*

Regular opportunities to practise debating skills in class will help students to develop confidence and experience in this field. Watching sample debates can also help to familiarise them with the format and key features. I tend to show video clips from chat shows, courtroom dramas or political debates; this enables students to identify key features of this genre of speech. It also provides a real setting and context for such tasks.

I use modelling techniques to demonstrate successful and less successful approaches. Get more confident students to help with this before starting to assess group performances. Supply less proficient speakers with opening sentences, including connectives or question stems, to promote discussion and give them the confidence to chip in, without relying on a pre-prepared script. I tend to allow students to rehearse their debates for the first few times they try something like this. More experienced or confident students benefit from preparing independently and then sparring using improvisation.

Drama-based tasks

◆ *Using interesting stimulus*

In my experience, the best drama-based approaches usually follow on from the study of an engaging and thought-provoking text such as a poem, song, story or media clip. Like any other task, students will get more fired up by the activity if they are intrigued by it, so try to develop role play tasks that will require students to develop interesting and challenging roles. The most successful role plays involve students using their imagination and empathy skills beyond the original stimulus text. For example, try staging a police interview with the persona from a poem, or an argument between two characters that never meet within the original text.

◆ *Developing role play skills*

It is important to remember that students are likely to have a whole host of role play skills that they can transfer from their drama lessons. However, there is a distinction between drama performances and drama-based speaking and listening. While aspects such as body language are important, students are assessed on the quality of their communication, so there is no need to get carried away with costumes and props. Also, remember that performing scripted pieces is not acceptable; students have to be responsible for their own speech, acting out a section of a play script will not meet the English criteria.

Drama strategies such as hot-seating (getting a student to act as a character and answer questions in role) and conscience corridors (students exploring a character's preoccupations by calling out thoughts as a student in role walks past) can be good warm-up activities to stimulate speaking and listening tasks.

Again, watching sample drama pieces to evaluate skills can be effective; I have successfully used exam board materials with students in the past – they enjoy watching students in other centres engaging in similar tasks, and are usually very perceptive when applying assessment criteria to other students.

◆ *Performing for an audience*

It is important that you remind students of simple performance techniques such as the importance of positioning your body towards an audience and projecting your voice, even if you intend to mumble or whisper in role. For drama-based assessments, it is crucial that students maintain the audience's interest by developing a complex character, therefore giving attention to aspects of presentation such as pitch, tone and levels. Encourage students to vary and develop these facets to show the nuances of a character through a range of interactions with others.

For this kind of task, I do think it is important to set up an appropriate performance space. If possible, it may be best to book out a drama base or school hall to give these activities enhanced status and gravitas.

Assessing speaking and listening

◆ *Capturing performance*

Recording students' speaking and listening performances with a video camera or dictaphone can be a great way to formalise the process and make it seem more professional. Students will be keen to stay in role and do their best if they know that the footage can be replayed and evaluated by themselves and others. If you wish to do this, make sure that you book equipment in advance and it is fully charged for use. Also, make sure that you know how to work it – many schools have a range of different cameras, each with their own particular functions. I often make a skilled student responsible for the taping so that I can concentrate on coordinating and assessing the performance.

Students can be wary of being on camera so I would only really use this method once I have built up a rapport with a class and developed their speaking and listening confidence. Although this approach can be a very helpful way of capturing the performance for assessment and feedback purposes, students may be stifled by the camera's presence and end up with stiff, false performances. Also, don't be reliant on the video footage as the only means of assessment; try to make some brief notes as well, just in case there are problems with transferring or saving the footage. Initially, I tend to walk around the class and give students one-to-one advice and feedback before expecting them to perform publicly.

◆ *Assessment and target setting*

As with any other aspect of English, students benefit from good formative assessment methods with speaking and listening activities. It is important to make students aware of the success criteria when preparing them for a task, and to familiarise them with specific level descriptors. Students tend to revert to a few very simplistic targets such as 'speak loudly and clearly' when prompted to think of their own; make sure that you prompt students to select more demanding objectives.

Assessing speaking and listening can be more challenging than other types of English response; many teachers rely on gut instinct instead of referring to specific criteria. The need to assess while the performance is taking place, rather than when you take books in to mark, also poses another challenge, especially when you are grading individuals within a group performance: you can end up frantically writing copious notes, preventing you from giving the students your full attention.

Try to develop a quick short-hand method of jotting down students' success and areas for development. I find that diagnostic tick sheets can help you to keep focused on the assessment criteria without having to write it out. One sentence of praise and one or two targets added to a tick list of skills exhibited is ample feedback.

◆ *Using peer and self assessment strategies*

Audience members can end up becoming quite passive and switched off when faced with a lesson full of speaking and listening presentations. I would recommend trying to involve the whole class in the task by giving audience members a specific observation role. Simply asking students to make a note of individual performances in the back of their books so that they can judge their favourites at the end of the lessons gives the whole class a focus. Further to this, I recommend dividing up the assessment criteria to groups within the class so that everyone focuses on a different aspect of the performance and has specific feedback to share. Designating time for peer review at the end of each performance also gives you, the teacher, time to complete assessment sheets and get organised for the next group.

I always provide scope for students to reflect on their own and others' performances. This helps them to identify specific areas of success and improvement and encourages them to engage with teacher feedback, not just their mark, grade or level.

Tool kit for teaching reading **6**

◆ *Reading for pleasure – challenging apathy and disinterest*

There are an ever-growing number of reluctant readers in secondary schools. With a host of other stimulating media forms battling for teenagers' spare time, reading for pleasure often loses out. Students who read very little, miss out on a lot. Not only do they deny themselves the exciting experience of investigating new worlds, learning new subject matter, exploring different experiences and imagining other lives, they are also likely to under-achieve.

We know that students who read regularly are likely to have improved comprehension skills and a better grasp of grammar and vocabulary. By promoting reading for pleasure, we are not only encouraging students to improve their literary appreciation, but are enhancing their chances of success, in English, across other school subjects, and in the future.

Regularly talking about reading and building in regular opportunities for students to read good-quality texts within their English lessons is important. Try to catch students young to encourage and extend their reading habits; many come from primary school with routines for private reading from the emphasis on the literacy hour and reading schemes. Unless secondary school teachers continue to make reading a priority, many students (boys in particular), will drop it in lieu of some other, seemingly more exciting, hobby.

Most of the time, children who don't read much claim that they don't know what to read, or that they don't enjoy fiction.

Many were obsessed with a particular author or series when they were younger and once they devoured that particular collection of titles, they found themselves at a loss. Weak students can also be put off reading because they don't have access to quality books appropriate to their reading level. Good links with the school library can be an effective way of introducing texts to students and encouraging them to explore the titles that are on offer. If students aren't given the chance to visit the library within lesson time, many won't make this trip voluntarily.

Providing recommended reading lists to parents can be an effective way of promoting reading at home. Reading challenge schemes such as the Readathon can add a sense of purpose and competition. Also, try to set interesting homework that involves independent reading tasks to give students an incentive.

◆ Developing students as critics

Building in opportunities for students to appreciate the craft of writing and share their opinions about the texts that they have read can help them to become judicious readers. Amid the 'can't read, won't read' culture in secondary schools, it is worth including discriminatory debate about texts so that students come to realise that it is OK to have preferences; just because they haven't enjoyed certain texts in the past, doesn't mean they will find all reading unenjoyable.

◆ Introducing a range of texts

Extract-based work has its place in English lessons and can be a good way of introducing students to a wide range of different styles, authors and genres. However, reading a whole text is an incredibly important experience for students and should not be saved for their Literature exam text in Year 11 alone. If students don't have access to reading materials at home, a class novel may be the only chance they get to read one from cover to cover. Against stereotypes, all students benefit from good quality children's literature; both genders can appreciate the war horrors in *Private Peaceful* and the relationship issues in *Dear Nobody*. Using shortlists from children's book awards can help to introduce you to popular and highly-acclaimed texts. Often reading a great book like *Holes* or *Millions* in school can actually inspire students to read other texts by that author and rejuvenate their interest in books.

It is also important to stress to students that all reading is good reading. While teachers and parents tend to favour classic novels in place of fashion magazines, skateboarding websites or car manuals, reluctant readers should be encouraged to read anything and everything that they are interested in. If students realise just how much they do read, this can help to break down their resistance towards the concept of reading, and their reluctance to engage with other texts.

◆ *Building up students' analytical skills*

A key skill in English is to be able to engage with a text beyond simply being able to read for meaning. If students are going to be able to deduce, infer and analyse the intricacies of texts, this is a skill that should be developed throughout their school career. Comprehension activities have become limited in the English curriculum, seeming rather old-fashioned. Many Key Stage 3 reading schemes are dominated by written responses that encourage students to write in role; while this does encourage empathy, the focus shifts to their writing skills, rather than the quality of their reading.

Try to build in analytical questions and essay-style responses from Year 7 onwards. By starting with modelling strategies and small, manageable tasks, students will become proficient at independently tackling challenging exam tasks by the end of Key Stage 4.

Comprehension skills

◆ *Selecting extracts*

Many teachers rely on textbooks and exam papers to develop students' comprehension skills. While these resources do provide useful extracts and accompanying questions, it can be off-putting for students to be faced with a large amount of text to read, followed by a number of difficult questions. Students can be tempted to rush through comprehension tasks when there are lots of questions to complete, so try to encourage them to engage with detail by keeping texts small and focusing on one specific aspect to respond to. Once students develop their comprehension skills and reading stamina they will be able to read longer extracts and complete a variety of questions in depth by themselves – don't expect them to be able to do this independently from the start. Like any other English skill, comprehension needs to be taught explicitly; merely practising questions or going through them as a class is unlikely to help students to develop this skill.

◆ Active reading methods

The key to developing students' independent reading skills is helping to make them active readers. All too often students adopt a passive role: they listen to others reading, sometimes read aloud themselves, offer an interpretation, but then wait for the teacher to confirm or explain the meaning to them. This is highlighted in GCSE revision classes where students are desperate to have lots of annotations endorsed by their teachers, treating their notes like security blankets, as though dutifully regurgitating these in their exam responses will lead to good grades.

You need to encourage all students to develop their own understanding of texts before sharing your own with a class. By providing time for them to think, respond and discuss their own ideas, you are enabling them to formulate individual interpretations of texts. It is also important to assert the validity and benefits of multiple readings so that students aren't anxious about providing the 'right' answer.

Good-quality questioning can help students to elicit their own understandings and meanings from a text. If classroom questioning is limited to simple comprehension, then you aren't giving students the chance to use their higher-order thinking skills. Asking students questions that will prompt them to evaluate, synthesise and analyse aspects of a text allows them to rehearse the kinds of skills that they will be expected to exhibit on paper.

Other active reading strategies include highlighting and note-taking; they can help students to identify main points and important language. However, it's important that students are taught how to use these methods; left to their own devices, some will highlight or copy entire passages. Again, modelling these techniques early on in Key Stage 3 will help students to develop the skill to discern the most significant points, words or text features.

◆ Addressing the assessment foci

By GCSE we expect students to be able to unpick the wording of comprehension questions to decipher the specific focus of the task: language, comparison, structure, audience, etc. However, before the final throes of exam preparation, often students will plough through comprehension questions without understanding what skills the task is expecting them to exhibit. Since many other subjects use comprehension questions to test students' memory of key concepts, it can be challenging for students to realise that it's not what they know and understand, but how they explain their knowledge that matters. Again, getting students familiar with assessment criteria early on can help them to appreciate what the questions expect of them. I would recommend focusing on one type of assessment foci at a time so that students can familiarise themselves with the format of the questions. The traditional method of working through an entire exam paper in a lesson should only be done for exam practice otherwise students can become overwhelmed by the different types of questions and may end up responding very superficially.

Non-fiction

◆ *Using real-life examples*

Using fresh and relevant texts such as newspaper clippings, magazine adverts and junk mail leaflets for comprehension purposes can help students to engage with the activity more than a page out of a textbook. Encouraging students to bring in reading materials from home can also help to keep the activity real and make them realise that they are surrounded by non-fiction texts that could be analysed in this way – they are not limited to reading materials found in comprehension tasks.

Another benefit of using these types of non-fiction texts is that students are more likely to appreciate that they have a real audience and purpose beyond the classroom. These materials can also be more engaging than black and white A4 copies of non-fiction texts; they come in a range of colours, textures and sizes.

◆ *Interrogating audience and purpose*

Another aspect of independent active reading skills is helping students to develop their own strategies for interrogating texts. When students are looking at an unseen piece of material, they should be encouraged to ask their own questions about it, such as:

- What type of text is it?
- Who is the target audience?
- What is the purpose of the text?
- What kind of language does it use?

◆ *Comparing different texts*

In preparation for the kinds of tasks that students will be expected to complete at GCSE and beyond, it's a good idea to get students used to comparing texts and evaluating their similarities and differences. Try to get them to draw thematic links between fiction texts, as well as selecting very different texts, to get students used to the idea that comparison can and should mean explaining the reasons for differences. Choosing similar text types or subject matter but very different approaches can be very fruitful. For example, comparing a range of websites that deal with the same issue, or a variety of adverts for the same product that are aimed at slightly different target audiences; this helps students to appreciate nuances and be sensitive to subtle differences, rather than making general and vague sweeping comparisons like adults vs. children, fiction vs. non-fiction, formal vs. informal.

The Media

◆ *Tips for using still and moving images*

Try to get students to appreciate media as texts in their own right, rather than as something fun that they get to consume or produce as a treat. With a generation of media-savvy teenagers it can be fairly easy to engage them in complex analysis of media texts, applying comprehension skills that they find challenging to exhibit with regular reading materials. Sourcing texts from the internet and scanning real examples of media texts is a good way of making use of popular, current and relevant media. Making use of free educational materials from media institutions such as Film Education, and others such as charities and commercial companies can also prove fruitful.

◆ *Reading media texts*

Model the kinds of interrogation that you would like students to exhibit with any other type of text: close textual analysis; insightful interpretation; perceptive evaluation. Students will start to see that looking at media texts is not just a reward or a hobby – they are expected to engage with still images or moving image clips at a sophisticated level.

◆ Useful terminology

It's a good idea to equip students with meta-language that will help them to analyse and deconstruct media texts. For example, if students can decipher diegetic sound (natural atmospheric sound) as opposed to non-diegetic (superimposed sounds such as voice-overs and soundtracks) this can provide them with the tools to explore the producer's methods, meaning and intentions. However, beware of plying students with a bulky list of terminology that encourages them merely to name the parts of a text rather than analyse effects in detail.

Poetry

◆ Introducing poetry

Poetry can be a daunting prospect for students, especially if it contains complex or antiquated language. The standard approach of reading a poem as a class and then discussing it to decipher its meaning and the techniques used by the poet can be a dry and tedious activity, serving to put students off poetry by making them feel as though they 'don't get it'.

Essentially, it's important to keep students interested in poetry beyond Key Stage 2 and this often means continuing to use approaches that are successful with younger students. Incorporating active strategies with poetry, like getting students to perform it, create pictorial presentations, or create their own poems in a similar style, helps students to engage with poetry and have fun with the language.

It's also important that you as a teacher show your enthusiasm for the poems that you study with your classes. While the syllabus dictates a substantial focus on poems, particularly for GCSE and A Level, you may be tempted to side with the reluctant students by responding to their groans or negativity with the 'I know it's dull, but we have to do it' argument. You will naturally have your own preferences and there will be certain poems that you don't appreciate as much, and I think it's good to share this sense of discernment with your students. However, your rationale for teaching poetry shouldn't be limited to fulfilling examination criteria; it's important to help students to appreciate poetry by modelling your enjoyment and interest.

Students will tend to search for the meaning or story in any text that they are faced with. With difficult poems – either pre-1914 texts in which the language or context is challenging, or with more modern, obscure or ambiguous poems – this can prove a barrier to students. Try to encourage them to appreciate poetry without necessarily fully understanding it. You could focus on the sound or the tone of the poem before exploring the meaning, or focus primarily on a specific quote or language feature.

Also, encourage students to create their own meanings from poems without jumping to give your interpretation of the texts. Examination students, in particular, can be anxious to ascertain the 'right answer' from the teacher – it is important that you make them realise that they are being assessed on the skills they exhibit in the exam, not the content of their ideas. Using exploratory methods when introducing poetry can help students to practise developing their own interpretations and justifying them.

◆ Interactive teaching strategies

One definition of poetry is that it is 'the best words, in the best order'. An effective method to encourage students to examine a poem's structure is to give them a chopped-up version for them to sort. It's important to stress that what is important with this task is the discussions that accompany the sorting process, rather than getting the correct order. With a poem like Martyn Lowery's, *Our Love Now*, students can gain huge amounts of insight into the themes and perspectives by focusing on the layout of the verses; the opening lines 'He said . . .' and 'She said. . .' generate the hypothesis that this poem is a balanced discussion in which the woman responds to each of the man's points. When the students' realise that in the original version, all four of the man's verses are intended to be read first, and are then followed by four verses from the woman, this encourages them to re-evaluate the poem's tone and meaning.

Chopping up poems can also make enjambment seem more pronounced. For instance, scrutiny of sections from Imtiaz

Dharker's, *Blessing*, helps students to appreciate the fractured presentation of the narrative and can highlight the impact that the structural devices have on the interpretation of the poem's meaning and effect.

Another simple method that can be used to emphasise vocabulary is to 'crunch up' poems. This involves presenting a page of words that have been taken from the text. Before students get embroiled in the narrative, this allows them to focus on the connotations of the words in isolation. They can also appreciate repetition and can devise their own ideas about the poem's themes in advance. For instance with *The Laboratory* by Robert Browning, focusing on the words 'poison', 'laugh', 'her', 'enticing' and 'drop' can generate some good speculative discussion about the events in the poem. It can also be helpful for students to identify unusual, complex or culturally specific words before they encounter them within the body of the whole text such as: 'prithee', 'phial' and 'filigree'.

Key to all of these approaches is building in time for students to discuss aspects of the poems in a supportive environment where they can experiment and not risk feeling foolish. It's important that students lead discussion and are not always looking to the teacher to find out what to say, think and feel about the poems: you should strive to develop a classroom in which reader response is paramount.

◆ Micro analysis

When students are asked to write about poetry, their temptation, as with any other text, is firstly to describe the content. When writing a comparative response, after they have summed up what each poem is about, some students may attempt to analyse quotes and comment on language effects. However, by this point, many students will feel exhausted by the page of narrative they have already written and won't have much time left to develop the quality of their response with detailed analysis. I would recommend focusing on the details first and foremost as a means of encouraging students to write more about less. Explain to students that teachers and examiners already have a working knowledge of the story of the poem – it's better for them to spend their time and energy exploring the effect of specific features of the text.

A good way of developing this approach is by modelling micro analysis with a specific word, phrase or textual feature. If you encourage students to get involved in class textual analysis from the first moment they are introduced to a text, rather than wait until they have studied it in depth, you will be developing this skill and making sure that it takes priority in students' responses.

I would also recommend analysing linguistic and structural features in isolation before students have had a chance to make sense of the whole text. For example, asking students to identify the use of verbs in *This Room* during the first reading, can help them to immediately appreciate how Dharker creates a sense of movement in the poem. Even before they have had time to explore the poem's meaning, the focus on the verbs may help them to identify a sense of chaos, panic or excitement. Approaching textual analysis with one method at a time also helps to provide focus and makes analysis manageable – the old-school approach of spotting as many techniques as you can and pausing to annotate and explain each one, overloads students with information and can distract them from appreciating the effect of specific poetic choices.

◆ *Embedding poetry in the curriculum*

Poetry can provide rich and creative lesson opportunities. I believe that poetry deserves a strong place in the English curriculum and that students should be able to appreciate a range of poems and poetic styles throughout their English career, not just as and when it's prescribed by exam syllabuses. Using anthologies of poetry throughout Key Stage 3 can enable students to develop the analytical and comparative skills that will be required of them later on. My long-term plans include Caribbean poetry in Year 7, Ballads in Year 8 and a comparative poetry scheme in Year 9, including themes of love, ageing and war. This gives students access to a wide range of poetry from different cultures, poets and time periods throughout their English studies.

As well as studying poetry in designated schemes of work, it's also a good idea to build in poems to complement and accompany the study of other texts and English skills. It can provide great stimulus for creative writing and role play; it can also be used to explore relevant themes, issues and language features. For example, I'd recommend looking at Liz Loxley's, *The Thickness of Ice*, when teaching extended metaphors; this poem has proven particularly successful alongside Berlie Doherty's novel, *Dear Nobody,* in which she also uses the image of ice cracking to suggest a fragile relationship between the central characters. Carol Ann Duffy's, *Stealing,* proves really effective as a stimulus for speaking and listening; students enjoy an interview-style drama activity in which pairs create an interrogation between the central kleptomaniac protagonist and an authority figure such as a police officer or social worker.

Making space on the calendar to celebrate events such as National Poetry Day and promoting poetry competitions can also help to raise its profile and gives students the chance to be creative. Each October the National Poetry Society publishes a theme for the day; previous topics have included work, food and identity. I recommend that you pause a scheme of work for a couple of lessons to explore the theme and associated poetry on it before helping students to create their own poems for display or performance purposes. The National Poetry Society and other institutions also run periodic competitions on specific topics; some publish anthologies of students' work. Building these competitions into your lessons can prove fun and rewarding for Key Stage 3 students to enter.

To avoid the potential mental block and blind panic that Key Stage 4 students face when attempting to write analytical essays about two or more poems, it's best to introduce this kind of task early on in Key Stage 3. While all year groups benefit from fun, active and creative strategies, they should also be developing the skills to write critically about the poems that they have been studying. Introducing analytical tasks with ample support such as discussion, modelling and scaffolding should enable students to build up their own poetry analysis throughout their secondary schooling career.

Prose

◆ *Teaching a class novel – how to cover a text*

Reading a novel with a class can be the most enjoyable aspect of English teaching: it allows you to experience the enjoyment that comes from reading a text in its entirety, and gives you the scope to explore the novel's themes, characters and structure in depth. However, the class reader also has the potential to lack the structure, pace and challenge that we expect from good quality

English lessons. To avoid tedious hour-long lessons filled with reading around the class, repetitive writing activities and predictable homework tasks, it's important that you give the teaching of a novel ample thought and planning.

Studying a novel with a class allows you to promote reading and extend students' literary horizons. With reluctant readers, it can also be an important way of demonstrating that books can be fun. While there are differences between studying a text as part of the curriculum and reading for pleasure, making reading enjoyable should be at the heart of your planning.

One really important decision is the text that you choose to teach. You may be fortunate enough to find your departmental stock cupboard brimming with exciting teenage reads, but it's more likely that you will have to jostle with colleagues for a dog-eared class set to avoid out of date or uninspiring novels. Try to be organised and plan in advance so that you can speak to whoever's in charge and procure a novel that you are happy to teach – this will have a big difference on your motivation to plan activities to accompany the text, and the enthusiasm with which you discuss it in class.

The level of reading difficulty, the length of the novel and the types of issues and content that it deals with, should also be factors for consideration when choosing a class novel. It may be tempting to plump for a text that you are really familiar with, perhaps one that you studied yourself for A Level or at university. While it's helpful to teach a favourite text, you should be basing your choice around the most suitable novel for the individuals you are teaching: a bottom set Year 9 studying *Far from the Madding Crowd* because you are a Hardy enthusiast and wrote your dissertation on the development of Bathsheba and Oak's relationship is not a sensible decision. Similarly, choosing to teach *Junk*, a novel revolving around narcotics abuse, because you want to engage students with a gritty narrative or because it was the only available text, is not going to curry favour at Year 7 parents' evening.

If you haven't read the book you are teaching before, then it's vital that you do this in advance to allow yourself time to generate teaching ideas and source and/or make appropriate resources. If you aren't careful you could find yourself reading ahead the night before your lesson and this is unlikely to give you enough scope to plan for decent and appropriate tasks.

Reading an entire novel with a class can prove challenging, especially if you are trying to cover 350 pages in a short half term. Rather than starting at page one and hoping that you'll have time to get to the end, it's advisable to be more pragmatic and plan to cover a designated number of pages per week. Break up the text into sections and decide what chapters you want to students to read in class and (stock and book policy permitting) what you would like them to read at home. Breaking up the reading in this way will help to make the text manageable and will avoid lessons becoming solely dominated by whole-class reading. I would also recommend breaking up the reading with appropriate activities that encourage students to reflect on and interrogate what they have just read. However, long spans of reading may prove entirely appropriate for a rainy afternoon when students are really enjoying a passage and you can sense that they are keen to read more.

◆ Strategies for sharing the reading

Reading to a class is a good way to model the features of effective reading aloud: volume, intonation, pace, enthusiasm, emotion. It's not only primary school children that enjoy having a story read to them; I have experienced GCSE classes completely absorbed by a teacher reading *Of Mice and Men* or *To Kill a Mockingbird*, especially if they are prepared to use a range accents. It may be tempting to read yourself every lesson to avoid having to select volunteers, or because you know that students' have weak reading levels and are likely to struggle or become frustrated with their own, or others, reading aloud. However, I think that it's important to build up students' reading confidence and stamina, and that group and class reading is possible with all classes if introduced and established effectively.

You will undoubtedly have keen and confident readers that will volunteer to read aloud each lesson; however I would avoid restricting the reading to a few individuals; as with teacher reading, this can lead to a large amount of students sitting passively just listening. However, forcing students to read in turn can result in conflict, refusal or embarrassment if they don't feel comfortable reading aloud. It's therefore important that you create a supportive classroom environment in which students aren't afraid to make mistakes with pronunciation, for example.

Introducing shared reading as part of a routine helps to make students realise that it's an expectation for all of them to get involved. I tend to start off the reading but tell students that I will be calling out names and asking them to continue, usually after each paragraph, depending on the nature of the group. Starting with short, easy passages can be less daunting; if reluctant readers only have to read one line they are less likely to refuse to participate. Another way of supporting weaker students is checking that they will be able to tackle the language in the extract that you expect them to read or even telling them in advance what you will be asking them to read so they can prepare themselves for this.

◆ Tips for administering books and homework

When reading a class novel, one of the trickiest tasks can be distributing the texts and making sure that you get all of them back in a good condition, especially if you are allowing students to take the books home. In this instance, it's really important to have a system so that you have an accurate record of who has what text – it's easy to lose a handful of texts each time to disorganised students who forget to hand them back in – and this will avoid wastage and causing a lot of inconvenience for yourself or a colleague the next time the text gets used.

Keeping novels presentable and well organised helps students to take pride and responsibility for the books. Hopefully, your department invests in plastic dust jackets to protect the book covers and replaces worn texts to keep stock looking fresh and appealing to read. Numbering texts and stamping them with the name of your school makes it easier to keep track of the texts and it's more likely that students will hand their books back in. When administering books, make sure that you make a note of numbers of novels that students have taken – I'd recommend recording these on a proper template or saving them electronically; if you just jot them down on a scrap of paper you are likely to lose it. Getting students to sign books out and in can also help to formalise the process and make the students take it more seriously. If your department has support from administrative staff, you may be able to use them to help you with organising texts by locating the books and preparing the paperwork in advance.

If you do choose to set reading passages for homework, try to build in strategies for students to record their reading and demonstrate their understanding of these. This will help you to check that students have completed their homework and will make the tasks more challenging. The obvious outcome is to write a summary of the chapter they have read, but you could incorporate some more inventive and interesting activities to accompany their reading homework such as writing in role, quizzes or selecting an important bit of language from the passage to explain in detail.

◆ *Planning to sustain variety and interest*

When you have a large text to study, it can be easy to resort to a formulaic lesson format in which most class time is spent reading long passages and pausing to discuss, with the odd empathetic writing task thrown in. While it's important to devote time to these types of activities, try to vary the content and style of your lessons to sustain students' interest and engagement with the text. Continue to plan good-quality four-part lessons with a variety of interesting activities revolving around the novel.

Using inventive and creative teaching ideas and resources such as music, video clips and speaking and listening discussions, can help to explore key themes and different issues found within the novel. Try to design writing activities that enable students to cover a range of purposes and styles, avoiding the temptation to repeatedly set letter- and diary-writing tasks.

It's really important to gauge students' focus and interest in the text and use this knowledge of the class to plan appropriate lesson activities. You may need to tweak your plans according to how engaged students are with a particular aspect of the novel.

Essay writing

◆ *Starting them young – introducing essay writing skills early on*

As I have already mentioned earlier on in this chapter, the key to developing competent and confident essay writers is to embed this skill early on in the students' schooling career. GCSE students often baulk at the term 'essay' because they find the process of structuring a sustained piece of analytical writing extremely difficult. There is no need for students to have such a negative experience – if approached in the right way, essay writing can becoming rewarding. Once students become familiar with the key features of an academic essay, by exploring different planning strategies and practising detailed analysis, the task becomes routine.

◆ *Active planning strategies and tips to remove scaffolding*

In an attempt to make essay tasks manageable, many English teachers develop essay plans to support students' writing. Scaffolding can come in many different guises: generic headings that students need to personalise and add detail to; instructions for what to include in each paragraph; opening sentences for students to complete. While these planning formats can help to dispel students' fear and have the capacity to model structuring strategies, if students are passively following a highly prescriptive recipe, then not only are you likely to create thirty identical responses lacking personal interpretation, you could also be making students overly reliant on teacher instruction for this kind of response. The former issue means that it becomes difficult to differentiate what the students actually understand; they are merely telling you what you have asked them to. The latter problem can undermine students' confidence with this type of task even further; they will expect to be spoon-fed *pro forma* on every other occasion, feeling unskilled or disinclined to create their own plans.

Rather than planning *for* the students I advocate planning *with* them; by creating a plan collaboratively on the board, students can see the logic behind the process. Being able to contribute content suggestions collaboratively can also empower students and give them the confidence to plan more independently next time. It's important that you make students more responsible for their own plans, and making it seem like an easy and logical process can help with this. Try to keep scaffolding skeletal in form so students have the responsibility of adding flesh to the bones.

Getting students to generate ideas and then structure them can also help them to discuss and think explicitly about the best form of essay plan. Try to focus on general skills that an essay should exhibit instead of getting bogged down in the minutia of essay content. Students should be taught to develop a good understanding of what makes an effective introduction, main body paragraph and conclusion, regardless of text and task; they will then be able to modify their plan accordingly.

◆ *Developing students' ability to analyse – PEE and beyond*

Most teachers rely on catchy acronyms to help students to

remember how to analyse. The most popular tend to be PEE (make a **p**oint, give **e**vidence and then **e**xplain the evidence) or PQE which emphasises the need for a direct quote. I know colleagues that make use of other memorable strategies such as using the metaphor of a hamburger (the burger is the meaty bit and the buns support it with explanation) or SEX (**s**tatement, **e**vidence, e**x**planation). I'm not so sure about the merits of the last example. However, telling students to PEE all over their work can make the term stick with them. The important thing is that students can do more than recall the technique – you want them to be able to use it effectively.

Often students struggle with the concept of explanation after they have provided some evidence – many resort to repeating their point again. It can be helpful to replace 'explain' with 'effect', thus prompting students to think about the impact that the selected quotation could have on the reader, rather than merely stating the obvious or, as is common with pre-1914 texts, attempting to translate the language into modern English.

◆ *Saying more about less – promoting detailed analysis*

I would encourage students to select a very specific and manageable quote for their evidence so that they can focus on detail to avoid wasting the time it takes to copy out a large chunk of text. Also, model deconstructing a quote in depth by picking out key words for further explanation; giving discussion time to this can also prompt a range of alternative interpretations. It's crucial for students to understand that the quality of analysis varies widely even when using the same technique; try to show them examples of a range of responses so that they can appreciate the difference between superficial statements and close textual analysis.

To support students in gaining higher grades, impress upon them the need to be discriminatory about their choice of points for analysis – there is no need for them to demonstrate everything they know about a text, they should pick the most salient features according to the focus of the task. Often students limit the quality of their responses by using a scattergun approach to analysis, moving quickly from one point to another; it's important for students to appreciate the need for substance and quality of explanation over the quantity of coverage.

◆ *Focusing on technique over content – strategies for analysing language, structure and form*

Students often fall into the trap of describing the text that they are studying; merely regurgitating the narrative to show knowledge of a plot will prevent students from achieving their potential. It is, therefore, important that you make this explicit. When writing about a novel, students tend to plan their paragraphs around key events or characters which can also tempt them into recounting rather than analysing. I find it's best to get students to focus on specific linguistic or structural features instead: this helps them to keep focused on the author's craft rather than lapsing into descriptive content. Selecting quotations for their paragraph plans also encourages students to revolve their analysis around specific textual details. Expanding one quote in depth can allow students to comment on a range of devices. However, it's important that students go beyond the mere naming of parts – focusing on explaining the possible range of effects that specific language examples can have will help with this.

◆ *Tips for effective introductions and conclusions*

Another thing that students find difficult is how to open and close an essay. For some, the difficulty in getting started can prevent them from making valuable use of lesson or examination time, sitting hopelessly trying to think of an opening sentence. Others may find themselves wasting time by rehashing the title for their opening paragraph, starting with 'In this essay I am going to . . .' and then stating the obvious, or by producing some overly generic or descriptive sentences that fail to gain them any marks. Conclusions, if students have time to complete them, can be equally pointless if students merely repeat all their main points or make a completely non-specific statement such as, 'To conclude, both poems have some similarities and some differences'. To ward against such pitfalls it's important to explore the features of effective openings and closings and to interrogate less successful examples to identify their limitations.

I suggest helping students to create a tool kit for introductory and concluding paragraphs that encourage them to demonstrate features from the mark scheme. For example:

Start by . . .
- Using a bold statement.

- Starting to answer the question.
- Including a personal opinion.
- Giving a specific example of a similarity or difference (if comparing texts).
- Focusing on an important quote

End by ...
- Exploring the author's intentions.
- Considering the effects on the reader.
- Including personal evaluation.
- Explaining the reasons for the similarities and differences (if comparing texts).
- Challenging the task/question and/or posing a new one

Exploring context

◆ *Ways to consider the author*

It's important that students explore a text through an analysis of the author's craft and intentions, rather than seeing a piece of fiction as a series of real-life characters and events. The teacher plays an important part in modelling this by speaking in terms of the author's intentions when discussing the text. It is also useful for students to have a working knowledge of the author's context to be able to apply this to their understanding of a text. You may wish to present relevant information to the class at the start of a unit of work, but I would recommend making this a research task for students to conduct independently, this way you are likely to get a wider breadth of information from a range of sources, and students can select the pertinent details themselves.

◆ *Strategies to research historical background*

For lower groups I would recommend providing a structured research resource to help them with their search for relevant biographical information. If you provide them with headings and questions you can avoid students copying and pasting from a website without engaging with the material. Also try to build in contextual details when studying a text, rather than looking at them in isolation; it is important that students discuss text and context together so that they are more likely to integrate background information appropriately within the body of their written response, rather than writing a potted biography in the opening paragraph before starting their essay properly.

Making explicit links to what students will have learned in other humanities lessons can help to make use of existing knowledge. For example relating the poem *Hurricane Hits England* to what they know about these natural phenomena from their Geography lessons or prompting them to use their historical knowledge of World War One and the Great Depression when studying war poetry and *Of Mice and Men*.

◆ Tips for engaging with cultural and philosophical context

By learning about a text's social and historical context, and finding out about the author's experiences and views, students will be able to surmise potential moral and philosophical messages. However, they are likely to need some prompting and support in order to consider doing this when responding to a text. The terms 'moral' and 'philosophical' may sound quite intimidating, but presenting this to students as 'the moral of the story' can help to put it into a concept that they understand from their experience of reading children's literature. Using media such as images and video clips can also help students to appreciate cultural context.

Getting students to share their perspectives of the issues and topics dealt with in a text can create interesting and varied debate, and this will help students to appreciate the multiplicity of interpretations that they can apply to a text. Incorporating speaking and listening tasks such as 'Ask the author' role play, or ethical debates, can also help to spark a range of ideas.

Tool kit for teaching writing

7

Principles for effective writing

◆ *Making the links between reading, speaking and listening, and writing*

Units of work tend to focus on one particular English skill but the best schemes and, I would argue, the best lessons, involve all types of skills. Speaking and listening discussions undoubtedly support the understanding of a reading text and can help to generate a range of ideas for a piece of writing. Likewise reading can act as a stimulus for speech and can also help as a model for writing tasks. Meanwhile, the act of writing often serves to demonstrate what students have learnt through their reading, listening or discussion.

Students tend to have strengths and weaknesses across the different English skills so it's advisable to provide a range of activities in a lesson that will allow them to engage and respond to the lesson content through a range of different mediums.

◆ *The importance of grammar*

Grammar periodically goes in and out of fashion within the English curriculum; as a result some teachers tend to be real sticklers for accurate spelling, syntax and punctuation, circling and/or correcting every error with angry ink, while others turn a blind eye to most mistakes, preferring to focus on the quality of students understanding and ideas instead.

The frequency and quality of the way in which grammar is taught also varies dramatically among English teachers. For some teachers, grammar exercises and tests are commonplace but for most, coverage and teaching methods are patchy. The old-school approach of teaching grammar in isolation is still evident in many English classrooms; while textbooks have generally become defunct, grammar worksheets or more whizzy interactive resources tend to be used within starter activities. However, where possible I would relate the grammar work to the written work students are engaged in, rather than treating it as a separate task; some students excel in spelling and punctuation tests, but then forget to apply this knowledge in their actual responses. It's important that students realise that accurate grammar should be a focus every time they put pen to paper, not just the reserve of one-off tests.

Deciding what grammatical features to focus on and how to teach them is problematic. In an attempt to cover curriculum objectives rigorously, you or your department may favour an approach which spreads grammar tasks across the course of a year indiscriminately, but I recommend that you choose features appropriate to the focus of your study. For example, learning about model verbs will complement writing to advise and doing a refresher lesson on possessive apostrophes is best done when you notice that students are having issues with that particular aspect of punctuation.

The most important thing is to keep grammar, and all other aspects of English language, in balance. Writing mark schemes do reflect the spread of skills that are required in a response, therefore avoid focusing on your bugbear at the expense of recognising all other successes and areas for development within a student's piece of work.

◆ *Developing students as writers*

In order to improve the quality of students' written work, it's crucial that they take the time to plan, prepare and then check their work. Students are often reluctant to do this, preferring instead to get straight on with the task in hand; therefore it's your responsibility to build in designated opportunities to focus on these crucial aspects of the writing process. Encouraging students to craft their writing by giving ample thought and attention to detail will pay dividends. Keep the focus on quality rather than quantity and include self and peer evaluation strategies to prompt reflection and editing.

◆ *Writing in different contexts*

Making writing feel real by giving students a clear sense of audience and purpose can also help them to take more pride in it. Using a range of topical issues and writing formats will help to spark students' imagination and sense of style. I've often had students wanting to send off their letters of complaint or persuasion addressed to celebrities, TV companies or politicians because they have become really engaged in the task. Developing creative and unusual activities such as a letter to space to explain life on Earth, or a speech to convince the rest of your year group not to download films illegally, have provided students with a fresh scenario with which to test out their writing skills.

Preparing for independent writing

◆ *Interesting stimulus and subject matter*

Using media texts or physical props can help to stimulate students' opinions or imagination regarding a particular topic that you want them to write about. Material such as news clips, music videos, or poetry can be shared with a class to promote discussion or ideas. Random objects such as shells or flowers can also help to generate students' thoughts. However, make sure students aren't allergic before you hand out mini chocolates or any potential irritants. Be inventive and imaginative to provide students with a range of leads for their own written responses.

◆ *Using examples of text types*

Showing students good and bad examples of writing can help to inform and shape their own writing. Looking at peer responses, either from the class or past students can be a useful way to evaluate writing style. However make sure that you are sensitive to students by asking their permission, blocking out names, when appropriate, and creating a positive climate of constructive criticism. Real-life texts can also help to set a standard for students' work, so try to source examples from newspapers, magazines or the web.

◆ Modelling strategies

As with reading responses, modelling the writing process can help students to learn skills and strategies to improve their writing. Either sharing the experience of writing from scratch with a class by explaining your word and syntax choices to them, or by getting students involved to construct a group piece, can be a powerful writing tool. What also works really well is taking a bland piece of writing and editing it together to improve the language and structure for effect.

◆ Allowing students choice

Students enjoy writing about what they know or what interests them so it's often a good idea to give them an element of choice so that they can select a task or subject matter to suit. This works well for differentiation purposes and can allow students to pick a suitably challenging task. It also makes students more likely to complete a task to the best of their ability if they have invested some of their personality into it, which is especially pertinent for homework completion.

Sentence structure and punctuation

◆ Accuracy and effect

When students are focused on the big picture – how and what they are going to write – it is often difficult for them to appreciate the importance of sentence structure and punctuation. Even top set students can be found omitting apostrophes or writing a whole response in simple sentences because they get carried away with the content of their written work, rather than the way in which they write it. It's important that students have a good working knowledge of the different types of punctuation and sentence structures for them to be able to use them accurately and experiment with the full range.

◆ Embedding new punctuation

Making sentence types and punctuation marks the focus of lesson starters is common in English lessons, but I also think it's crucial to make this an explicit focus when you are reading other people's texts so students can appreciate how they are used in context. Once students are clear about how to use a range of punctuation and sentence structures, they can start to focus on the effect of specific authorial choices and mimic these in their own writing.

Since mark schemes allocate a substantial number of marks to this area, it's important that students get the opportunity to learn about this aspect of the English curriculum and practise their use of these devices. If you teach the semi-colon, for instance, try to make using this new piece of punctuation a target for the students' next piece of writing, and the focus for your assessment of that work.

◆ *Experimenting with sentence structures*

One good strategy for highlighting sentence structure use is getting students to rewrite short passages using a range of different forms, in an attempt to make the original version more effective. By focusing on the effect of sentence level choices you are emphasising the need for students to reflect on how they are constructing their writing, instead of spending all their energy on the content.

◆ *Allowing time to craft writing*

Encouraging students to pay great attention to detail in order to craft their written responses requires time: often students are keen to hurry ahead and complete a task, but by making students slow down the process and consider the nuts and bolts of their writing, you are helping them to develop and hone their skills, instead of repeating the same style each time they write. This kind of approach will help students to take more pride in their responses and promotes the need for thinking, planning, proofing and editing time.

Composition and effect

◆ *Developing awareness of audience, purpose and style*

When reading, it's important for students to have a good sense of audience and purpose to make sense of the writing style. It's good to emphasise this element of composition so that when students are doing their own writing, they focus on the target audience and purpose in order to write in an appropriate style. When setting tasks, make sure that you outline a clear sense of audience and purpose. Furthermore, when you are preparing students for exam tasks, encourage them to interrogate the questions for the target audience and purpose.

Most students have rather a simplistic grasp of audience, purpose and style. They may generalise target audiences, for example only differentiating between big demographic groups, e.g. adults, teenagers, old people, without appreciating that target audiences can be much more specific than this, e.g. homeowners with young families, teenage girls keen to keep fit or well-off elderly people who enjoy luxury holidays. You may also need to highlight that texts can have multiple target audiences: an article in a school magazine may be read primarily by students, but teachers, parents and even local members of the community may be additional consumers. Try to encourage students to consider this in terms of primary and secondary audiences. This concept may help them to consider the content and style of their own writing more thoughtfully.

If students are familiar with the writing triplets, they should be able to identify the purpose of a task with ease. However, not all questions will explicitly use the words inform, explain, persuade, etc., so students will need to become adept at interpreting tasks to understand the intended purpose. Students also need to appreciate that, just as a task can have multiple audiences, it may also address more than one writing purpose. For example, writing a report to your boss to update them on a project may be writing to inform and explain, but it could also be an attempt to persuade them that you are competent for the task; it might also include advice or suggestions, depending on the context.

It's also important to develop students' understanding of writing style beyond the formal/informal dichotomy that many of them are limited to. Modelling the more subtle nuances such as being aggressive, witty, objective, personal, etc., will help students to broaden their understanding of style and enable them to experiment and adapt their writing more successfully.

◆ Extending vocabulary

One key aspect of developing students writing to a more sophisticated level involves helping them to extend their vocabulary. Avid readers or students that are used to lively and sophisticated debate at home are likely to have an extended vocabulary, but it is necessary to help students to apply more complex words appropriately in context. For many students, their main strategy for broadening their vocabulary is using a thesaurus when typing up their homework. Exchanging synonyms can help students to acquire new vocabulary, but it can also be quite a passive activity where students trust the computer to select a suitable word. It can also lead to a great deal of malapropism if students opt for an inappropriate alternative.

Modelling wide vocabulary use in your own lesson, through discussion and writing can help students to acquire new words. Choosing texts with more sophisticated word use can also help. Rather than hoping that students acquire new vocabulary purely by osmosis, make it the focus of your learning objectives when appropriate. When marking drafts of students' work, identify repeated words or phrases and encourage them to exchange them with more interesting and wide-ranging vocabulary.

◆ *Evaluating writing effects and sharing 'best bits'*

To avoid students becoming reliant on your feedback and guidance to improve their writing, build in opportunities for self and peer evaluation. Getting students to read each other's work can really help to promote reader interest, even if it's just skimming through one paragraph. I encourage students to share best bits, rather than reading out whole responses to the rest of the class. This makes students prioritise and select the most effective passages; it also enables more students to get involved in peer review, rather than this becoming the domain for only the most confident or able members of the class.

Text organisation

◆ *Modelling writing structures*

As mentioned in the chapter on essay writing, it's important to support students' writing by sharing helpful strategies for structuring their ideas, but you mustn't become too prescriptive. Students' need to take ownership of their writing and this won't be possible if they are made to feel as though there is a correct format that they need to adhere to. The opposite approach of leaving students to get on without any guidance can leave them feeling lost at sea, and also does little to help them to improve their skills.

With non-fiction writing, teachers tend to put modelling and scaffolding strategies into practice; demonstrating how to organise and write an argument, a letter or an article. However, there tends to be a wide range of approaches when it comes to creative writing, ranging from complete independence to very detailed formulaic writing frames. I think it's important for students to be offered a range of tools and approaches for all types of writing, both fiction and non-fiction. Again, it's the teacher's responsibility to choose an appropriate approach to support students without being overly rigid and dictatorial. This way, students will be able to develop their writing repertoire without having their creativity stifled.

◆ *Planning and proofing strategies for creative writing*

Generating generic writing frames together can help to provide students with a template for their written work which they can personalise to meet their own needs. Offering model plans, opening lines, or examples to improve and adapt, can also be helpful, depending on the nature of the class members and their needs. I find the GIG CAR model to be quite a helpful and flexible strategy for helping students to plan a short story:

> **G**rab the readers' attention;
> **I**ntroduce an issue;
> **G**ather pace;
> **C**reate a climax;
> **A**nticipate ending;
> **R**esolution.

If you don't provide any direction of guidance for tasks like poetry or story writing, assuming that students will have the capacity to generate their own responses, you may find less confident or creative members of the group floundering. Meanwhile, without instruction or challenge, other members of the class may be merely regurgitating the same quality of writing as they were achieving in primary school.

Many students are reluctant to spend time planning and checking their work properly in order to prioritise writing their response. Once of the reasons that they avoid this is because they don't know how to do it properly and feel as though it's not crucial; it's important for you to instil the importance of these two processes and the positive effect that they can have on the quality of students' work. Teaching these skills explicitly will help students to incorporate them as part of the writing process. Using writing time effectively in order to build in space for planning and checking is also important.

Helping students to know what to look out for when they are proof-reading will help to make this a useful and purposeful activity; often students read through work so quickly that they miss obvious errors and waste the opportunity to tweak and improve their writing. Try to model proofing practices with one focus at a time, otherwise it can be overwhelming. Slowing down the checking process helps students to identify syntax, grammar or spelling mistakes. Encouraging them to read again with an eye for improvement shifts the focus to the quality of sentence structures, vocabulary and punctuation choices. Highlighting words or phrases for development when marking can help to direct students in this process.

◆ *Using topic sentences and sign-posting*

When reading texts, examining the opening of each paragraph helps to identify the writer's argument. Students should also be taught to focus on the quality of topic sentences when completing their own responses. Writing these first, straight after the plan, can help students to develop a logical flow of ideas. Some students will need help in realising that they don't need to write 'In this paragraph I am going to...'; there are better ways to signpost their response for the reader. Meaningful use of connectives can help with this process. Spend lesson time focusing on the range of phrases that they could use to link together their ideas, but be wary of students peppering their responses with empty comparisons, merely using 'however' or 'on the other hand' without going on to outline specific similarities or differences.

Spelling strategies

◆ *Grouping spellings*

Teaching spellings can be tricky because students are necessarily going to have different capabilities. With so many words to tackle, it may also be difficult to know where to start. I would recommend focusing on spellings that are particular to the topic of work your students are studying; supplying a bank of words for them to learn and use with their writing. For example, when teaching letter writing skills, the words 'faithfully', 'sincerely', and 'enclosed' are likely to prove useful and relevant. Also, covering words with the same spelling rules together can make the task manageable.

◆ Spelling tests

Spelling tests are a traditional way of gauging students' spelling skills. This is still a good way of motivating students for learning new spellings and many students enjoy the competition and rewards involved. Testing without prior notice can help you to see how much students know – I would encourage you to retest with the same words to allow students to tackle mis-spelt words.

◆ Personal spelling strategies

While whole-class spelling tests can help to introduce new words, many students will have different spelling issues. Encourage students to keep a record of their own personal spelling errors for learning. Highlighting or circling mistakes may help students to identify them – you may wish for students to use the back of their exercise books, or another book, to use the 'look, cover, write, check' technique. Encouraging students to create their own mnemonics to remember tricky spellings can help, e.g. '**a p**ea makes a good **parent**' to remember the spelling of 'apparent', as can getting them to break down a word into manageable chunks, e.g. 'sub-terra-nean'. Having easy access to a set of dictionaries in your lessons, and prompting students to look up tricky words for themselves, can also help to develop students' spelling.

◆ Spellings in context

While it's good to give spellings their own focus in your lessons, it's no good if students can spell in isolation after revising for the purpose of a test, but don't spell accurately within their written responses. Teaching spellings that link to a scheme can help students to make the connections. Slowing down the writing process and encouraging students to check their work carefully can also help to highlight the importance of accurate spelling.

However, avoid emphasising spelling skills at the cost of all of the other writing skills; students and parents in particular, can become blinkered and overly critical of poor spelling. While accurate spelling is important, it does only count for a small proportion of mark schemes, and it can be demoralising for students who struggle with spelling. It is better to keep this skill in context of all the others, to avoid students sticking with safe words rather than experimenting with new, more sophisticated vocabulary in fear of getting it wrong.

Teaching the writing triplets

◆ Exploring real texts

Making use of brochures, newspapers and websites can help to model a variety of writing styles for students. Making explicit links between reading and writing will enable students to identify the features of different writing styles. For example, before asking students to create their own piece of advice writing it's good to scrutinise the language, structure and tone used in a real-life agony aunt article to help students to locate and explore the effect of features such as modal verbs, empathetic writing and the use of suggestions. Regular contact with a variety of examples really helps; once students start to appreciate the various forms of writing and their common ingredients, they can start to use these in their own responses.

◆ Identifying features of specific writing styles

The twelve writing styles are usually organised into triplets within exam tasks which can help students to appreciate commonalities between the forms:

> Inform/explain/describe – detail
> Analyse/review/comment – scrutiny
> Persuade/argue/advise – opinion
> Imagine/explore/entertain – imagination

When you have identified common features within the triplets, it's then a good idea to explore the difference between them. For example, how 'writing to inform' usually depends on facts and an impersonal style, whereas 'explain' has an emphasis on causality and justification, and 'describe' can make use of features of fiction writing, e.g. imagery and description.

One useful activity is getting students to focus on a particular topic but present it in different ways, depending on the writing purpose. For example: an informative brochure about the school; an article explaining the benefits of a good education; an imaginative piece of description about a deserted school.

◆ Writing for a real audience

Assigning an actual audience for students' writing can help them to adopt an appropriate style for the task. For example, a letter to their favourite celebrity persuading them to attend a school's charity event, or an article for the school magazine arguing for free periods for Year 11 students. Making it seem like a valid audience will motivate students to write with purpose. Even better, provide students with an actual motivation to write, such as a competition entry or a letter of application to a work experience provider. With the emphasis on functional English, we have a clear responsibility to help students write for practical purposes.

Being a highly organised and efficient English teacher

8

Principles for effective organisation

◆ Being productive

With such a heavy workload, English teachers can't afford to waste time – you will need to develop a range of strategies to tackle planning and marking productively so that you accomplish your to-do list and achieve a healthy work–life balance. It's easy to find yourself working late nights and for a large chunk of the weekend, and at key crunch points in the year you may find it necessary to do so. However, long working weeks need to be addressed, otherwise you will become tired and unproductive and this is likely to have a converse effect on your work rate and your ability to function effectively at school.

◆ Feeling in control

Many teachers adopt a passive approach to their job, moaning about an unrealistic and demanding workload as though they are bound by their to-do list; it's important to feel in control of your tasks and this starts with prioritising your workload and making decisions about how much time you can afford to spend on each task. Following the advice that we give students about managing homework and planning in advance pays dividends, otherwise you will find yourself taking in an unrealistic amount of marking, or working incredibly long hours to meet report deadlines. Also, acknowledge that just because a teacher's work is never done, it doesn't mean you shouldn't stop; you could

111

always do more and better, but if you want to remain sane and happy, and you value your relationships with your friends and family, you cannot afford to.

◆ Feeling successful

Feeling in control and working smarter, not harder or longer, can really help with job satisfaction. It's important to get a sense of accomplishment and pride from your work so make sure that the way in which you organise your time and priorities will allow you to accomplish this. Setting achievable success criteria for yourself is part of this realistic process: it's no good trying to mark every page of every exercise book in detail if you only manage to look at four books in an hour and have to give unmarked books back the next day because you ran out of time and/or fell asleep while marking – this will only serve to make you feel demoralised and out of control. Make sure that you use your time effectively and to good purpose so that you can experience the joy of triumphantly ticking items off of your to-do list instead of feeling guilty and useless because you haven't managed to achieve the inordinate amount of tasks you had planned.

Managing time

◆ Tips for avoiding time wasting

Time management is crucial in all of this; as teachers don't have enough time to complete the endless amount of work to the standard they would like, it's even more crucial that you make the best use of the time that you do have.

Beware of people who sap your energy and time; while it's important to develop good working relationships with your colleagues, and this does necessitate time to catch up at the end of the day or during a break, avoid getting into a rut with certain individuals who regularly off-load their problems on to you, taking up half an hour of your time when you could be doing something more productive. When starting off in teaching you are likely to want to chat about your day with others, but limit this time to perhaps ten minutes after the bell and then get into a routine that involves working somewhere you can be undisturbed, or heading home for some peace and quiet.

When you are tired, you may find yourself particularly

unproductive, wasting time doing easy, pointless, non-urgent jobs to guard against more taxing items on your to-do list. Be more self-aware of this – if your brain has switched off then you are probably better off having a proper rest or going for a brisk walk, rather than staring at a blank screen or busying yourself with something unnecessary.

◆ *Tips for prioritising and cutting corners*

Knowing what job to do next will require you to apply some thought and self-discipline. Some teachers, like many students, leave things to the very last minute and are always fire-fighting by tackling the very urgent tasks. However, if you are always in a rush to complete tasks to a tight deadline you won't really give them the time and thought that they deserve. You may also be causing yourself to be in a permanent state of stress and anxiety if you are constantly working to a tight deadline. Keeping a clear sense of all of your tasks and their level of importance and urgency will help you to keep an overarching picture of your priorities and goals. Stand back from tasks to decide what they require of you and when:

Non-urgent/important	Urgent/important
File the task and create a clear deadline for completion. Set yourself interim reminders and, if it's a large task, break it down into manageable chunks. Build in time to consult with others if appropriate.	Act immediately because it won't take much time, or prioritise time in the near future to get this task completed. Ensure that you create clear reminders for yourself and seek assistance from others if necessary.
Non-urgent/not important	**Urgent/not important**
Decide whether these tasks actually need doing at all; if not, don't waste your time. If they do require some kind or action or response, consider delegating to someone else, such as administrative support. Even if you choose to do nothing, keep a record of the task if you think it may prove useful in the future.	

When you lack experience, it may be difficult to know what corners you can afford to cut and how you even go about this.

Use colleagues' expertise to find ways of saving time. This may involve sourcing ready made resources, or borrowing approaches that will help you to accomplish more in your working day.

◆ Dealing with perfectionism

Many teachers seem to suffer from acute perfectionism. I have experienced this at stages in my teaching career and still have bouts every now and again, but in order to maintain a realistic, healthy and manageable workload, it's important to acknowledge and accept that you haven't got the time or energy to be as perfect as you would like to be. Some of the tell-tale symptoms of this condition are below:

- Meticulous planning in which the extra time spent preparing your lesson outweighs the benefits experienced by students as a consequence of your labour.
- Endless tinkering to perfect resources to the point of spending hours trawling through Google images to find the right picture to accompany your worksheet.
- Laborious marking that involves writing copious notes in students books – if you are writing more in response to students' work than they did themselves, this is a bad sign.

Watch out for these behaviours and modify the way that you work to keep tasks more manageable. Assign designated time to mark a set of books and aim to stick to a few minutes per student – writing reams is only off-putting and overwhelming for students anyway, so it's better to prioritise the marking of one particular assignment and feel like you are doing this properly. Again, when developing lesson plans and resources, have a time goal for the task and stick to the time that you have committed. While taking thought and care with your planning is important, over-thinking your lessons can actually be counter-productive; sometimes teachers get so embroiled in the preparation of a lesson they forget the important aspect is actually the delivery and how you engage the students. Also, if an activity does go belly up, you will find it far more crushing if you have spent hours painstakingly creating the accompanying resources. Try to stay rational about the whole process and don't whip yourself into frenzy around needing to be perfect; this will only serve to cause you stress and anxiety, which is not conducive to a confident teaching persona.

◆ *Effective use of non-contact time*

As I emphasised earlier, your time is precious so use it wisely. Teachers' designated planning, preparation and assessment (PPA) time is grossly insufficient for completing everything required of us, but many teachers fail to make good use of their protected non-contact time in school. An hour block isn't very long to get stuck into a set of marking or tackle a lengthy to-do list, but if planned and used effectively, you can accomplish a range of small tasks in this time or make a dent into your workload. Some teachers choose to mooch around the staffroom in their free periods having an extra cup of coffee and chat with colleagues. On occasions, where you are exhausted and need a break during the day, or would benefit from catching up with someone, there is nothing wrong with this. However, if you find yourself lapsing into this pattern of behaviour every time you are free, try to address it, otherwise you are wasting a large time of potentially productive time.

I would recommend planning your free periods in the same way that you plan your lesson time – select tasks from your to-do list to fit into this time, such as photocopying, calling a parent, or doing some marking. If you don't create a particular focus or purpose for this time, you may end up squandering it. Again, it's important to find somewhere to get on with your work uninterrupted during your free time. If your classroom is used for another lesson, choose an office or find a free classroom that you can use for the hour.

Avoid relying on free periods to get crucial things done at the last minute; if you are pulled away for emergency cover, or the photocopier needs a new toner in the non-contact time you had planned to use to plan and prepare for the following lesson, you will find yourself in an awkward situation.

◆ *Setting and meeting deadlines*

There are many deadlines to be met in the school calendar, such as reporting stages. However, you will have lots of personal deadlines among these published ones relating to your own classes and timetables, mostly dominated by planning and marking.

It's important to stagger your workload and set realistic and achievable deadlines for task completion. If you merely meander through tasks, not fully clear about how much time you can afford to spend on them, you are likely to be unproductive and miss important deadlines.

Managing tasks

◆ Strategies for keeping a to-do list

It's important to develop a system or recording and tracking tasks that you find helpful and easy to use. Many teachers prefer to keep a paper copy of a to-do list, crossing out and adding to the list throughout a week. Some prefer to keep this list electronically so that they can completely delete accomplished tasks and keep the list looking neater and more professional. The most important thing is that your preferred format is handy, useful and easy to use. Writing separate tasks on post-it notes can prove useful as you can stick them to your desk or planner to remind you of specific tasks – you can also have the satisfaction of scrunching them up when the job has been completed. In order to achieve that feel-good feeling, I know of colleagues that actually add finished items to their to-do lists so that they can get a sense of accomplishment from crossing them off. Conversely, be wary of adding tasks to the list that you have no intention of doing, otherwise they will stay on your list while other jobs come and go, making you feel like a failure for not tackling them.

◆ Tips for keeping organised

Having an organised work space can help you to keep a clear mind. For some teachers, being militant about clutter and adopting a clear desk, pigeon-hole and in-tray policy is what they need to do to feel in control and on top of things. Others manage very successfully in a perpetual state of organised chaos – looking as though they are drowning under unyielding piles of paperwork, but being able to find everything they need at their fingertips if they need to. Most teachers strike a happy medium, knowing that there is scope for a tidier classroom but not being prepared to spend hours meticulously filing. The following are some basic principles for keeping yourself and your environment organised:

- Throw away or recycle things that you don't need – this will save space and avoid hiding important things that you need with clutter that you don't.

- Designate areas for different types of paperwork and resources – this will help you to locate what you are looking for, especially if it's been a while since you last used it.
- Keep a notebook for key reminders or actions – this will help you to keep all *aide-memoire*s in one location, rather than following a paper trail of scruffy notes on individual scraps of paper.
- Dedicate some time at the end of each day for clearing your work space – this will help you to feel organised and will avoid you having to face a jumble of papers in the morning.
- Invest in folders or trays to separate work handed in from different classes – this will help to prevent work becoming merged with each other.
- Create a filing system that is easy to manage – if you have to hole-punch sheets or place them in individual plastic wallets before filing away you are less likely to do it.

◆ *Delegating tasks*

Since the workforce reform agreement, there has been an increased focus on teacher workload and more money invested into administrative support roles in school. By being more organised, you can make better use of the support on offer. Planning photocopying, display work or other types of administration in advance, gives you the chance and time to delegate the task to someone else. In many schools, booking work through reprographics ends up cheaper than photocopying yourself, but often colleagues leave it too late to arrange this. Getting students to help with tasks can also be effective. Form members that arrive early in school are often quite keen to help out with organising resources in exchange for merits or other rewards. If you have prefects, you may be able to make them responsible for displays, for example.

Managing marking and paperwork

◆ *Dealing with post*

Try to deal with correspondence immediately, to avoid handling post, e-mails, invoices, etc., more than once. Sort out post the moment you take it out of your pigeon hole and this will prevent you from taking a pile of assorted mail to your classroom to deal with later – the likelihood is that this pile with grow and become

even more unmanageable. Having an in-tray on your desk in which to keep pending correspondence is a good idea – you can then keep track of important items amidst all of the other paper in your classroom. However, beware of filing important documents away, never to be seen again – it's easy to forget about things once your brain thinks that you've organised them and therefore you have dealt with them.

◆ Avoiding paper mountains

To avoid an avalanche of paper flowing over the edges of your desk, try to cut down on the paper that you accrue in the first instance. By cutting back on photocopying and storing sets of resources within envelopes or folders, you can help to keep papers organised and manageable. Letting filing build up can create untenable piles of paper – try to create a quick and easy filing system that will prevent this from becoming a big issue.

◆ Keeping your work space organised

As I've already intimated, a tidy and organised work space can lead to a happier and more efficient approach to your work. You need to make sure that your classroom has designated storage space that you can utilise for your benefit. You should have drawers, cupboards and/or filing cabinets in which to store and save reusable materials or important documents. Set up these spaces to suit you so that is easy and effortless to put things away. Labelling drawers or setting up boxes, drop files or ring binders in which to store resources can help.

◆ Tips for getting coursework sorted

With the sheer volume of coursework the average teacher handles on a yearly basis, it is hardly surprising that it is commonplace for individual pieces to get lost. It's imperative that you have a rigorous system for collecting and storing coursework to prevent this from happening and from warding off accusations from students and their parents that you are responsible for the loss. Having a folder or box for all coursework from a particular examination class can help you to store the work centrally, especially if individual pieces are handed in late; if you don't have a specific place for the work, you have a higher chance of losing it among another pile of work.

Keeping an accurate record of work that has been handed in is also important. You may wish to print off a class list to annotate and keep with the pile for your reference; you may prefer to keep an electronic copy of this. To allay the possible conflict, you could get students to sign work in and out so that you have an undisputable record of who has got the work. With less reliable individuals, I photocopy marked first drafts and keep these to avoid the risk of students losing all trace of their coursework due to their haphazard organisation.

Managing stress

◆ *Recognising personal stress triggers*

Teaching and nursing are recognised to be two of the most stressful professions. With demanding workloads, challenging behaviours and highly-regulated timings to stick to, it's hardly surprising that a high proportion of teachers suffer from stress, to varying degrees, at points in their careers. While a hectic job like teaching is likely to create stressful situations, you should not accept a state of worry and fretfulness as the norm. Since prolonged experiences of stress can lead to serious conditions such as depression and other anxiety-related illnesses, it's important to recognise when you are feeling particularly stressed and attempt to regulate this.

Often we feel stressed when we feel out of control, either with students, peers, workload or home life. If you know that a particular cohort of students or a member of staff has the capacity to wind you up and increase your stress levels, try to anticipate and diminish this effect, either by confronting the behaviour that is causing you distress, or changing the way in which you process such experiences.

◆ *Keeping perspective*

You are likely to encounter many sources of potential frustration within an average working day at school. Try not to allow yourself to get sucked into negative interactions that will cause you to become anxious. Teachers tend to be very passionate about what they do, but avoid expending all of your energy into one particular issue, conversation or work task – to meet the demands of your day you need to feel fresh and ready to tackle what you are faced with, instead of drained and mentally exhausted.

As much as this is a cliché, remember it is just a job and however difficult or challenging a situation you find yourself in, in the grand scheme of things it isn't worth your health or happiness. Furthermore, you will find it far more difficult to deal with a tricky student, parent, colleague or task in a professional manner if you are wound up, as this is likely to make you irrational and overly-sensitive.

◆ Tips for avoiding burn-out

To avoid exhausting yourself by working too hard and/or worrying excessively, try to clearly differentiate between work and play time. Many teachers, especially in the early stages of their career, allow their work to eat into their spare time. This is often necessary, but it's important that you make a reasonable chunk of your free time sacrosanct. If you find this difficult to do, try leaving your laptop and work at school on designated evenings so that you can enjoy your free time better, knowing that there is nothing for you to be getting on with.

Knowing your limits and keeping track of your workload and tiredness levels can help to keep your work–life balance in check, but ultimately you need to make time for other priorities in your life such as family, friends, hobbies and personal time to yourself.

◆ Developing stress-busting strategies

When bogged down with work, especially on a dreary winter's day in the middle of a long half term, it's easy to lapse into unsociable working patterns which can make you despondent and depressed. Make sure that you inject fun, enjoyment and opportunities to unwind into your working week to avoid this. Some tried and tested ideas for keeping positive and tackling stress:

> *Exercise:* The links between physical and psychological health are scientifically proven. Try to build in time to stretch your muscles and exert your body rather than your mind. If you are not particularly sporty, a brisk walk in the fresh air will do you good. You may find aggressive, high adrenaline sports a good way of letting out some steam. Something gentler, like swimming, can prove therapeutic and relaxing.
>
> *Singing and dancing:* On their own or together; letting your hair down can be a great way to release some tension. Learning a new skill, such

as salsa, can also help you to invest some time in yourself.

Do something creative: Playing an instrument or doing something artistic can help you to concentrate on something other than your school work.

Laughter: Don't underestimate how much laughing can combat stress and help you to gain perspective of a situation.

Reading: Despite the fact that a love of literature is what brought many of us into the teaching profession, most English teachers manage to read very little during term time – build in time to get stuck into a good book at evenings and weekends.

Socialising/having fun: However busy you are, make sure that you still make the time to spend quality time with friends and family.

Eat well: When busy and stressed it can be easy to skip lunch breaks or rely on ready meals in the evenings – make time to eat properly and prepare decent meals.

Pampering/chill out time: Allow yourself time to veg. out and be unproductive once in a while. For many teachers Fridays are sacred for relaxing – make sure that you have pockets of time to focus on yourself.

Getting away: Despite having a great deal of holiday, many new teachers end up spending most of their holidays catching up from the last half term or planning for the new one. Even if money is tight, try to arrange to get away, even if it's just to visit friends or relatives; this will help you to have a proper, undisturbed break.

◆ *Sharing your anxieties*

Sharing your problems or concerns is not admitting failure. What is causing you stress may well be the effect of miscommunication or poor working practice; speaking to a line manager or colleague about what is concerning you could help to eradicate the problem, or give you ideas or strategies for solving it. Offloading problems at home can help to get issues off your chest, as can talking through what is concerning you, but beware of dominating your conversations with friends and families with issues from your day. However much they love and care for you, incessant moaning is not an attractive quality and if you are finding yourself repeatedly talking about the same anxieties, then this is a clear signal for you to address these issues at work.

Organising resources

◆ Developing an effective filing system

As I've already mentioned, setting up a sensible filing system can help you to store resources quickly and easily. Having systems in place, such as labelled folders, can minimise the hassle and time it takes to file documents and resources.

◆ Strategies for storing resources

See what works for other people, and what doesn't. I would recommend keeping master copies electronically so that you don't have to worry about filing a paper master copy. A logical system of folders and sub-folders for each scheme of work and class can help you to direct files into the correct location so that they can be easily retrieved later on.

◆ Keeping track of resources

Giving electronic files sensible and detailed names will help you to search for them easily. If you have a logical approach to filing you should be able to reach for allocated drop files, folders or boxes to locate resources. It is easy to lose track of resources in a hectic teaching schedule, especially if you are moving between classrooms or sharing resources with others. Try to store loose sheets within folders so that they are kept organised and all together. If you lend a resource to another member of staff, try to make a note of this, otherwise you are likely to forget.

Making the most of ICT

◆ Tips for being techno-savvy

Picking up shortcuts can save you a lot of time when producing resources electronically. For example, 'control s' for save, 'control c' for copy and 'control v' for paste. Incorporating hyperlinks into resources and schemes of work can help you to locate and open files immediately. This can be easily done by selecting text, right clicking and inserting the document or internet address that you want to link to. Lots of ICT skills can be learnt though trial, error and experience, but it helps to share tips with colleagues and make friends with ICT support technicians in order to develop your ICT know-how.

◆ *How to cope when your laptop crashes*

Having an ICT glitch in the middle of a lesson, especially when you are relying on a projected resource, can be a stressful experience. Even if you have spent a great deal of time, thought and energy developing a resource, if everything goes wrong, try not to panic and fall to pieces. Although it's highly inconvenient, try to patch over the situation by writing up key instructions on a regular whiteboard so that the class can continue with the lesson. Most of the time, shutting down your computer and starting it again will resolve your ICT issue but it's a bad idea to make a class sit and wait while you try to fathom what is wrong with your computer. Be prepared to abandon a resource if technical difficulties get the better of you. What's most important is that you keep the lesson going and keep the students engaged and working.

◆ *Strategies for minimising paper*

Beyond keeping paperwork and resources organised, try to reduce the amount of paper that you keep. While collecting resources is an important thing to do when you first start out in teaching, try to be discriminate about what you choose to keep. It is easy to leave a meeting with a heap of paperwork that you are unlikely to look at again – only try to take things that you find useful. When possible, save electronic copies of resources and avoid printing documents unless it is necessary. Be prepared to recycle or throw away materials that you do not need.

Being reflective and developing your practice 9

Principles for effective continual professional development

◆ Being relentlessly self-improving

When training to be a teacher you are continually striving to meet standards and prove your competence. The first two years of teaching involves a great deal of professional development, reflection and improvement; however, without continually striving for self-development, it easy to get stuck in particular ways of doing things. Try to step back from your workload to give yourself time to evaluate your strengths and weaknesses, and ways to improve.

◆ Looking for development opportunities

The traditional model of professional development involves seeking external INSET opportunities that match your areas for development. However, the quality of courses on offer differ immensely, and you may find that even if you do secure funding to attend, they offer poor value for money. One-off training events for individual teachers tend to have little long-term impact on teaching and learning back in school. Sourcing local training opportunities can be cheaper, more practical and also offer the capacity for networking with colleagues from other local schools. You can also learn a lot from teachers in your own school; organising some peer observation, team teaching, or time after school to share skills, can be far cheaper and more effective.

125

◆ Leading your own career development

You are required to keep a professional folder as evidence of your teaching skills and experience when you first start teaching. Try to keep this habit going beyond your NQT year – it's a good way of cataloguing successes and will help you to keep an up-to-date CV and collate evidence for threshold applications later on.

Ward against getting bogged down in the minutia of your teaching at the cost of losing focus of your own career development. Even if you don't consider yourself to be particularly ambitious, it's important to keep abreast of educational developments and continue to improve your own practice. Regularly evaluating your own strengths and weaknesses can help you to seek opportunities for further learning.

Evaluating lessons

◆ During the lesson – ways of gauging whether learning objectives have been met

The most important time to evaluate how a lesson is going is during the course of it: if you get the impression that students are struggling with what you have planned to do, would benefit from spending time on one particular aspect, or by doing something differently, then be flexible enough to respond to this accordingly. If you have invested a great deal of time planning a lesson and creating accompanying resources, then you may be reluctant to come 'off plan', but remember that a plan should support learning, not act as a straitjacket.

◆ After the lesson – time to reflect

If you have adapted your lesson plan during the course of a lesson, it is worth reflecting why and how you did this, and whether you can learn from the adaptations, i.e., could the scheme of work be tweaked or added to for the future. Although formal lesson observations become rare practice after your ITT year, avoid losing this reflective aspect of your teaching practice: simply thinking through a lesson and considering what worked well and what didn't work with the class can help you to reconsider your approach and learn from it.

◆ *Evaluating with others*

For many teachers, opening up their classroom for criticism can be a daunting experience. This is mostly because peer observation becomes such a rare act for the average classroom teacher and becomes synonymous with inspection and judgement. Early on in your teaching career, having other teachers in your lessons is a fairly common experience. Beyond your NQT year, try to continue peer observation practices; although it is no longer obligatory, except for performance management purposes, you will continue to learn a great deal from colleagues' feedback or lessons.

Professional development

◆ *The power of lesson observations*

Peer observation can be an enormously powerful tool for teacher learning, both for the observer and the observee. Creating professional dialogue based upon the common experience of a lesson can really help you and your colleagues to evaluate and fine-tune your teaching repertoire. Many schools and departments have systems in place to allow you to pair up with other teachers for observation purposes as part of continuing professional development (CPD) entitlement. Some schools take this one step further and have coaching triads and lesson study models whereby teachers are involved in peer planning, observation and evaluation. However, even if your school doesn't have formal peer observation practice in place, there is no reason why you shouldn't seek your own opportunities to observe other colleagues and invite others to do the same.

◆ *Recommended INSET*

Internal CPD opportunities such as twilight courses and training offered on INSET days provide a regular top up to your professional learning. However, the quantity of INSET you can expect to receive in a school year can be fairly tokenistic – many schools use CPD time to focus on administrative meetings in which information is transferred and decisions are made. External CPD courses can also be patchy in content and coverage. For many teachers, getting a day out of school and a nice lunch is motive enough to apply for an INSET course, but it's important that you research what's on offer before committing your time and the schools' money. Schools receive a vast quantity of INSET leaflets; if you feel as though you would benefit from external training in a particular area, discuss this with your Head of Department and ask them to recommend an appropriate course.

Stick to reputable and recommended training providers and look into the programme for the day. From personal experience, courses led by examiners or endorsed by your exam board can be the most useful. Research the names of the course leaders to investigate their background and experience in order to gauge how relevant the course will be. Also try to opt for training courses that involve practical activities; you don't want to set up cover for the day and travel into London only to have a PowerPoint presentation read to you, and leave with a pack of uninspiring paperwork.

◆ *Other CPD opportunities*

Getting involved with initiatives can be a great way of learning on the job, rather than listening passively to an INSET presentation. If your school has working parties or a teaching and learning group, try to get involved. Working collaboratively with colleagues within your school or a local partnership can have a direct impact on your classroom teaching and is more likely to cause sustained, long-term improvement than a one-off training course that you went on by yourself.

Other opportunities outside of school such as working on a pilot strategy project with the local authority can prove to be a fruitful learning experience, as can gaining experience as a GCSE examiner. The training for marking exam papers is comprehensive and can help you to become familiar with the success criteria. This can be of great benefit for your teaching and can help you to become much more confident with your own assessment practices.

Sharing and developing excellent practice

◆ *Sharing successes and failures*

When training to become an English teacher you are expected to be open and honest about your strengths and weaknesses;

failures are seen as an evitable part of the learning curve. However, post-NQT year, many teachers become more guarded about sharing their teaching experiences. Yes, in passing, many staff let off steam about something that is frustrating them, share an anecdotal experience or mention something that has gone well, but the quality of these exchanges tend to be quite fleeting and superficial: teachers don't want to risk to be seen as gloating or admitting weaknesses.

Being confident in your teaching should enable you to be open and honest about it. Mentoring sessions within your ITT and NQT year are a good forum for these kinds of discussions, but beyond that I would recommend you finding opportunities to talk about your teaching with like-minded colleagues, warts and all.

When starting out in teaching you tend to be modest: accepting others' advice, suggestions and criticism without feeling as though you have the expertise to return the favour. However, most English departments benefit enormously from having a new member of staff in the team; your fresh perspective, new ideas and keenness to develop resources will permeate through to colleagues and help the department to improve practice.

◆ *Avoiding becoming stale – risk taking*

Complacency can come with experience. When you get to the stage where you feel competent and confident, it is easy to fall into cyclic routines; regurgitating lesson plans year upon year, you can sometimes feel as if you have been teaching on autopilot. While there is a lot to be said for the familiarity and assurance that comes from re-teaching a topic, you should always look for new and interesting ways to deliver it, rather than relying on what you have always done in the past. To avoid reaching a plateau with your teaching, be perceptive and open to new strategies; take measured risks with your classes, rather than sticking to tried and tested lesson formats. When you start to feel like an 'old hand' avoid the temptation to become self-reliant – continue to learn from those around you, including the next cohort of trainee teachers.

◆ *Networking*

Having links with colleagues in other schools is another good way of sharing effective practice. Sometimes departments can become insular; since all schools ultimately deliver the same curriculum, it makes a great deal of sense to swap good ideas and resources. I'd recommend keeping in touch with colleagues that you trained with; these contacts may prove really useful in the future when you want to introduce a new course of study, visit another school for observation purposes, or learn about each others' successful teaching approaches or resources. It can also help you to gain understanding of local schools that will prove useful if job opportunities arise.

Developing your career

◆ *Keeping a record of your achievements*

Within the hectic fray of teaching it can be difficult to log your successes, but this is worth doing. Something as simple as having a folder in which you can stash any evidence such as thank-you cards from parents or colleagues, copies of exam results, a programme from a school production that you co-directed or an attendance certificate from an aspergers course, can all help to form a portfolio of your experiences. Having a folder in 'my documents' and your email inbox called 'my CPD' can also be an effective way of saving electronic evidence of your achievements. You may wish to set up a more detailed filing system with different sections for student progress, professional learning, etc., but as a bare minimum, having all of your data in one easily-retrievable location will be enormously helpful.

◆ *Getting what you want – tips for being assertive*

Within schools there are many different types of personalities. When you first join a school you are likely to keep your head down and get on-side with students and colleagues. However, just because you are the newest member of staff, doesn't mean that you have to grin and bear everything. Make sure that you do play an active part in department meetings and have a chance to get your voice and opinions heard. I'm not suggesting that you are bolshy and opinionated – this is only likely to lose you friends and alienate people – be tactful and professional at all times. Avoid public confrontations; instead choose an appropriate time to approach a colleague or line manager with a suggestion, or about an issue that is concerning you.

◆ *Getting recognition for your work*

Make sure that you aren't fobbed off with excuses or unreasonable work demands, just because you are new; it is unlikely that colleagues will consciously take advantage of their seniority or experience, but if you are keen and enthusiastic you may find yourself targeted by colleagues who want to make the most of your goodwill. Be selective about what extra jobs and responsibilities you take on, especially if they are not rewarded with any extra time or money. Learning how to say no is a key skill that you need to learn quickly to avoid drowning underneath an unreasonable workload.

◆ *Finding out what makes you tick*

When starting out in teaching you are already likely to have preferences for different parts of the English curriculum and you will probably be asked to audit your subject knowledge to identify areas of need. Furthermore, as you gain teaching experience, you tend to find certain aspects of the job more rewarding and enjoyable than others. This might be teaching Shakespeare to low-ability boys, developing students' creative writing skills, or using speaking and listening to generate discussion and debate. While it's important to develop your subject knowledge and teaching repertoire so that you have a balanced skills base, it's also good to become an expert in a specific field. Try to play to your strengths and make use of your expertise when contributing to schemes of work or teaching projects.

By going beyond the notion of strengths and weakness and actually exploring your own motivations, you can start to think about what you enjoy about the job, not just what you should be better at. This can help you to understand and overcome obstacles and help you to consider how you want your career to pan out and what you would like to be able to do more of. For example:

- do you find the pastoral elements of your job the most rewarding?
- does teaching Key Stage 4 give you the most job satisfaction?
- would you like to have more experience of supporting students with special educational needs?
- does your expertise lie in teaching A Level?

These kinds of questions could help you to identify particular roles and responsibilities that you would enjoy the most.

Organising English enrichment opportunities

10

The importance of developing English skills outside of the classroom

◆ *Planning educational trips*

Theatre trips to see texts in performance used to be a fairly common enrichment opportunity within English departments. However, the time and responsibility involved in organising educational trips has unfortunately put off many staff. Completing rigorous paperwork, including financial forms and risk assessments, does make this a laborious process, but it is ultimately worth the hassle: students benefit greatly from learning outside of school. The experience of seeing a performance of a Shakespeare play at The Globe, exploring the Museum of Film, Photography and Television, or witnessing live performance poetry at *Poetry Live* have undeniable benefits for the students and teachers involved. Outside the confines of the classroom, students can appreciate texts in a different way. The fun and enjoyment involved can make the experiences memorable and significant for students and also serve to refresh and invigorate staff.

However, I would warn against biting off more than you can chew. Try to get experience of school trips by volunteering to accompany others, even if they are being led by a different department. This will give you the opportunity to shadow the trip leader and take note of the way in which they organise the itinerary, students and staff. If and when you feel ready to lead your own trip, try to do so in partnership with another more experienced colleague so that you can get help with the process. Also, try to keep the activity small and manageable – a week-long residential abroad with the majority of year group would be rather over-ambitious for your first experience of organising a trip.

There is also lots of scope for arranging in-house educational visits. There are many touring drama companies or artists who can come into school to perform set texts. While you lose the fun factor involved in going out of school, this may be a more practical and feasible option for getting larger groups of students involved in such opportunities at a reduced cost and risk.

◆ *Organising extracurricular opportunities*

One-off educational trips and visits can be very rewarding and beneficial for students, as can regular clubs and activities within school. If your department already has extracurricular activities on offer, try to get involved by volunteering your services. If clubs are rather thin on the ground at your school, consider starting up one of your own by yourself, or preferably, with the support of a colleague. Lunchtime sessions allow more students to get involved, but depending on the length of your lunch hour and the nature of your teaching timetable, it may prove impractical to offer extra activities during break times. If you wish to start up a club after school, make sure that you look into school protocol regarding this. Some suggested activities include:

> *Reading groups:* These tend to work best when you have a specific focus for discussion. Shadowing a book award is good way of exploring good-quality books without having to create your own reading lists. I'd recommend the Carnegie award for both Key Stage 3 and Key Stage 4 and adult awards such as the Man Booker for A Level reading groups. Using the school library as a meeting point provides a calm and purposeful atmosphere for discussion. Providing refreshments is also a good idea. Students can post reviews, set up their own blogs or make links with other schools.

> *Debating clubs:* Check out what kinds of debating competitions take place in your area. Most provide topics for discussion and direct you to stimulus material that you can use to practise students' speaking and listening skills and prepare them for regional debates.

Student magazine: Budding journalists and skilled designers will enjoy being able to get stuck into a school publication. This may take some effort to set up if you want to produce a quality product. You will need publishing skills to pass on to students, and access to computer equipment. To cover printing costs and be able to circulate the magazine you will need to secure funding and reprographic support. It could also be published on the school internet.

Competitions/fundraising: Many charities and literacy organisations run frequent competitions that students can engage in to get their skills recognised and/or raise money for a worthy course. For example, the Roald Dahl Foundation and CLIC Sargent organise a yearly readathon to raise money for children suffering with leukaemia and cancer. Mencap organise school spellathons. Occasions such as World Book Day and National Poetry Day are normally accompanied by writing competitions that students can get involved in to win prizes and/or get their work published. Increasingly, media institutions such as the *Financial Times* and *Film Education* run competitions to get teenagers involved in writing about topical and pertinent issues.

Coursework catch up/revision workshops: In the lead up to important deadlines, students benefit from getting extra support from specialist staff. You may choose to run an after school coursework clinic for your own classes, or extend this invite to a whole year group. Closer to the exams, many students and their parents will be appreciative of extra revision classes where you can offer more one-to-one support. I'd advise checking out what other subjects have on offer and on what nights, so that you don't find yourself in competition for student attendance.

With all of these suggestions, success and longevity of the activities depend on the quality of publicity, promotion and information given about the activities. They also rely on staffing and teacher enthusiasm. Consider how you are going to invite students to get involved. Using assemblies and student bulletins to spread the word is a good idea, but a more personal touch can also prove effective. For example, suggesting a club to an individual that you think would benefit from it. Actually sending out invitations through registers or via home is also a good way of motivating students to get involved, especially if parents are aware of what is on offer.

Having time for a life outside school

Showing an interest in other aspects of students' experiences and interests, in and out of school can help you develop better relationships with them. Accompanying individuals on a school trip or watching them in an after-school sports fixture or production can help to develop rapport and show that you are interested in them beyond the context of your English lessons.

Making time to do extracurricular activities with and for students can be rewarding, but it's more important to make sure that you invest time into your *own* life outside of school. Due to the demanding, time-consuming and often exhausting nature of the teaching profession, it's easy to allow your energy to get sapped away, leaving you good for nothing at the evenings or weekends. It's important that you prioritise your own hobbies, interests and relationships to make sure that your life outside school is happy, healthy and satisfying. Ultimately this will benefit your teaching and your students. First, they will realise that you do have a life and a personality beyond your teaching persona. Second, you will be more relaxed and fulfilled as a consequence. Third, without a healthy work–life balance you are likely to become tired, moody, stressed and, more than likely, cynical about your job. Furthermore, a conversation about last night's England game, a newly-released film, or a gig or TV programme that you made time to see, is more likely to engage students' interest then bragging about the amount of time you spent planning and marking for their lessons. Yes, teaching is a vocation and you've got to care enough about it to make this challenging job worthwhile, but don't forget to lose sight of your own needs and best interests.

Resources

Quick glossary of terms

AfL	Assessment for learning.
AST	Advanced skills teacher.
Attainment targets	These define the knowledge, skills and level of understanding that pupils of different abilities and levels of maturity are expected to have by the end of each Key Stage.
BECTA	British Educational Communications and Technology agency: the UK government's leading Agency for information and communications technology (ICT) in education.
BT	Beginning teacher: a teacher who is working in a school as part of their initial teacher training (ITT).
CACHE	Council for awards in children's care and education.
CAL	Computer aided learning: applies to any learning experience that has been enhanced or supported by the use of computers.
CATs	Cognitive ability tests: an assessment of a range of reasoning skills.
CEDP	Career entry and development profile: used by all new teachers to chart their progression through their teaching career.
CPD	Continuing professional development.
CPO	Child protection officer.
Core subjects	English, maths and science: as part of the National Curriculum, all pupils must study these subjects up to Key Stage 4 (age 16).

CRB disclosure Criminal records bureau disclosure: it is a legal requirement that all teachers are checked against CRB records to determine their suitability to work with young people.

Curriculum The range and content of subjects taught within school.

DCSF Department for Children, Schools and Families. Formerly known as the education and children's services department of the DfES. Government department that regulates all areas of education and the National Curriculum.

Differentiation Differentiation involves teaching the same curriculum to students of all ranges and abilities using teaching strategies and resources to meet the varied needs of each individual.

DT Design technology.

Diagnostic testing A form of assessment that highlights specific areas of strength or weakness.

E2E Entry to employment: schemes and training opportunities working in partnership with schools and local authorities to provide suitable life skills, education and training to pupils who may have been excluded or gained very few qualifications.

EAL English as an additional language.

EAZs Education action zones: based around primary and some secondary schools. Support can include: school-home support workers, extra-curricular activity centres, homework support groups in local libraries and so on.

EBD Emotional and behavioural difficulties/disorder.

EdPsyc Educational psychologist.

EMA Education maintenance allowance: a fortnightly payment of up to £60 for students who are aged 16–19 who stay on in education after they reach the end of their compulsory schooling.

EMAG The ethnic minority achievement grant: government money for supporting schools and local authorities to meet the educational needs of minority ethnic pupils.

ESOL English for speakers of other languages.

EWO/ESW Educational welfare officer/social worker: a

| | | | person responsible for ensuring pupils' regular attendance at school and other related issues. |

GCSE — General Certificate of Secondary Education: the national examination that students usually take in several subjects at age 16.

GNVQ — General national vocational qualification: courses in vocational subjects such as art and design, health and social care and so on.

G&T — Gifted and talented.

GTC — General teaching council.

GTTR — Graduate teacher training registry.

HMI — Her Majesty's Inspector of schools employed by Ofsted.

HoD — Head of department (sometimes known as head of subject).

HoY — Head of year (group).

ICT — Information and communications technology.

IEP — Individual education plan: a programme of support for pupils with a statement of special educational needs.

In loco parentis — Means 'in place of a parent'; the legal term defining teachers' responsibility for pupils in their care.

INSET — In-service education and training for school staff.

ITT — Initial teacher training: the period during which a teacher undertakes training to achieve qualified teacher status (QTS).

Key Stages — The National Curriculum is divided into four main stages:

	Key Stage 1	Key Stage 2	Key Stage 3	Key Stage 4
Age	5–7	7–11	11–14	14–16
Year groups	1–2	3–6	7–9	10–11

LA/LEA — Local authority/local education authority: a division of the local government with specific responsibility for education.

LSA and LST — Learning support assistant and learning support teacher: support staff for pupils with special educational needs, often works with individual children in class or within designated learning support units.

LSU — Learning support unit: a department within a

	school set up to help students with learning and/or behavioural difficulties.
MFL	Modern foreign languages.
NT	National tests (formerly standard assessment tests SATs): tests used to show your child's progress compared with other children born in the same month. Tests taken at Key Stages 1, 2 and 3 cover the three core subjects; English, maths and science. GCSEs are taken at the end of KS4.

Key Stage	Age National Test taken	Published
1	7	No
2	11	Yes
3	14	No
4	16	Yes

NLS	National Literacy Strategy.
NNS	National Numeracy Strategy.
NQT	Newly qualified teacher: a person in his or her first year of teaching who has successfully completed their teacher training.
NRA	National record of achievement: a personalised folder detailing a student's achievement and attainment throughout their (secondary) school career.
Objectives	Goals, results or improvements that the decision maker wants to attain.
Ofsted	Office for Standards in Education: the organisation who is responsible for school inspections and assess the quality and standards of education.
PANDA	Performance and assessment: a report generated by Ofsted to allow schools to assess their performance and make comparisons with other schools nationally.
PAT	Pupil achievement tracker: a piece of diagnostic and analytical software produced by the DCSF/DfES to enable students' performance and attainment to be tracked.
Pedagogy	Refers to the art or science of teaching, but also describes the strategies, techniques and approaches that teachers can use to facilitate learning.

Performance tables	The collected statistics for schools and local authorities such as results of national examinations and absence data and so on, published by the DCSF.
PPA	Planning, preparation and assessment: at least 10 per cent of every teacher's timetable should be free for PPA time.
Programmes of study	The content of teaching programmes laid down in the National Curriculum for each subject.
PSE or PHSE	Personal and social education or personal, social and health education.
PSP	Personal support plan: personalised targets to support pupils often on the verge of exclusion
PTA	Parent/teacher association.
QCA	Qualifications and Curriculum Authority, the body that develops the curriculum and its assessment.
QTS	Qualified teacher status: qualification gained after successfully completing a period of teacher training needed to work in any state-maintained school.
SEN	Special educational needs: a term used to describe a range of conditions within three main categories: learning difficulties, behaviour difficulties or physical and medical difficulties.
SENCO	Special educational needs coordinator: the teacher with responsibility for SEN pupils within a school.
SMART targets	Specific, measurable, achievable, realistic and time-related: helping to monitor how targets and goals viewed and completed.
SLT	Senior leadership team.
SMT	Senior management team: the leading members of a school or education provider.
TDA	Teacher Development Agency, also know as Training and Development Agency for Schools (formerly the TTA – teacher training agency).
TLR	Teaching and learning responsibilities: responsibilities that impact positively on educational progress beyond the teacher's assigned role.
VAK	Visual, auditory and kinesthetic learning styles model refers to the preferred learning style of an individual and focuses on 'active' teaching and learning strategies.

Education and government

Department for Schools, Children and Families (DCSF)
⌨ Sanctuary Buildings, Great Smith Street, London SW1P 3BT
☎ 0870 000 2288   💻 www.dcsf.gov.uk

Department for Education in Northern Ireland
⌨ Rathgael House, Balloo Road, Bangor BT19 7PR
☎ 028 9127 9279   💻 www.deni.gov.uk

HM Inspectorate of Education (HMIE)
⌨ Denholm House, Almondvale Business Park, Almondvale Way,
Livingston EH54 6GA
☎ 01506 600 200   💻 www.hmie.gov.uk

Office for Standards in Education, Children's Services and Skills (OfSTED)
⌨ Royal Exchange Buildings, St Ann's Square, Manchester M2 7LA
☎ 08456 404045   💻 www.ofsted.gov.uk

Scottish Executive Education Department
⌨ School Education, The Scottish Government, Victoria Quay,
Edinburgh EH6 6QQ
☎ 0131 556 8400   💻 www.scotland.gov.uk/Topics/Education

Welsh Assembly Government Education and Skills
⌨ Minister for Children, Education, Lifelong Learning & Skills, Welsh
Assembly Government, Cardiff Bay, Cardiff CF99 1NA
☎ 0845 010 3300   💻 New.wales.gov.uk/topics/educationand
                              skills

What is a LA?
In England and Wales, local authorities (LAs) are responsible for managing all state schools within their area. Responsibilities include funding, allocation of places and teacher employment. You can locate your local authority via DSCF: www.schools-web.gov.uk/locate/management/lea/fylea

What are GTCs?
The General Teaching Councils are independent professional bodies with statutory power to advise the government on teaching. All qualified teachers in the UK working in state schools are required to register with a GTC.

GTC for England
- Whittington House, 19-30 Alfred Place, London WC1E 7EA
- ☎ 0870 001 0308   💻 www.gtce.org.uk

GTC for Northern Ireland
- 4th Floor Albany House, 73–75 Great Victoria Street, Belfast BT2 7AF
- ☎ 028 9033 3390   💻 www.gtcni.org.uk

GTC for Scotland
- Clerwood House, 96 Clermiston Road, Edinburgh EH12 6UT
- ☎ 0131 314 6000   💻 www.gtcs.org.uk

GTC for Wales
- 4th Floor, Southgate House, Wood Street, Cardiff CF10 1EW
- ☎ 029 20550350   💻 www.gtcw.org.uk

Teacher training

Administration
Graduate Teacher Training Registry (GTTR)
Responsible for processing applications for PGCE and PGDE courses in England and Wales, and Scotland.
- Rosehill, New Barn Lane, Cheltenham, Gloucestershire GL52 3LZ
- ☎ 0871 468 0469   💻 www.gttr.ac.uk

Training and Development Agency for Schools (TDA)
Government agency responsible for training and development of teaching workforce.
- 151 Buckingham Palace Road, London SW1W 9SZ
- ☎ 0845 6000 991   💻 www.tda.gov.uk

Training routes

Who needs QTS?
Anyone wishing to teach in a state school in England and Wales needs to achieve **Qualified teacher status (QTS)**. All the training routes shown lead to QTS or equivalent.

There is no QTS in Scotland, however, new teaching graduates are required to complete an induction year and register with the GTCS.

Bachelor of education (BEd)

An honours degree course in education. Courses enable students to study for their degree and complete initial teacher training at the same time. A popular choice in teaching primary school children: ⏱ 3–4 years.

Graduate teacher programme (GTP)

Trainees are employed by a school as unqualified teachers. On-the-job training is tailored to individual needs: ⏱ 1 year.

Postgraduate certificate in education (PGCE)

Trainees spend at least a third of their time studying at a higher education institution and two thirds on three or more teaching placements in local schools. Teaching placements usually last from two to seven weeks: ⏱ 1 year.

Postgraduate diploma of education (PGDE)

Similar to a PGCE, but followed by students in Scotland: ⏱ 1 year.

Registered teacher programme (RTP)

Training route for non-graduates, providing a blend of work-based teacher training and academic study, enabling trainees to complete their degree and qualify as a teacher at the same time: ⏱ 2 years.

School-centred initial teacher training (SCITT)

Trainees spend more time training in the classroom and are taught by experienced, practising teachers. Training is delivered by groups of neighbouring schools and colleges. May also lead to PGCE: ⏱ 1 year.

Teach First

Programme aimed to encourage top graduates to consider teaching as a career. Trainees work in challenging secondary schools receiving teacher and leadership training, as well as work experience with leading employers: ⏱ 2 years.

Pay and conditions

How does a new teacher's salary grow?

Newly qualified teachers are placed on the **main pay scale** (salary scale for classroom teachers in Scotland) at a point dependent on relevant career experience. Salary increases by one increment each year subject to satisfactory performance.

England & Wales: main pay scale (From 1 September 2008)

Spine Point	Inner London	Outer London	Other
M1	£25,000	£24,000	£20,627
M2	£26,581	£25,487	£22,259
M3	£28,261	£27,065	£24,048
M4	£30,047	£28,741	£25,898
M5	£32,358	£31,178	£27,939
M6	£34,768	£33,554	£30,148

What is the STRB?
The **school teachers' review body (STRB)** reports to the Secretary of State for Education making recommendations on teachers' pay and conditions in England and Wales.

What about teachers in Northern Ireland?
Teachers' pay scales in Northern Ireland are generally the same as those in England and Wales.

Scotland: Salary scale for classroom teachers (From 1 April 2008)

Scale Point	Salary
0	£20,427
1	£24,501
2	£25,956
3	£27,432
4	£29,025
5	£30,864
6	£32,583

What happens when you reach the top of the scale?
In England and Wales, teachers who reach the top of the main pay scale can apply to cross the 'threshold' and move to the upper pay scale. In Scotland, teachers can apply to become chartered teachers when they reach the top of the salary scale.

Unions

Should I join a union?
Union membership is strongly recommended. Teaching is a demanding profession with many potential legal minefields. Teaching unions provide legal and professional advice, guidance and support.

What are the benefits of TUC affiliation?
Most unions are affiliated to the trades union congress (TUC) and members benefit from being part of a larger organisation. Independent unions typically cater for more specialised professions and are not bound by inter-union agreements or political affiliations.

Association of Teachers & Lecturers (ATL)
Represents teachers and lecturers in England, Wales and Northern Ireland. TUC affiliated.
- ✉ 7 Northumberland Street, London WC2N 5RD
- ☎ 020 7930 6441   💻 www.atl.org.uk
- 👥 120,000

Educational Institute of Scotland (EIS)
Largest organisation of teachers and lecturers in Scotland. TUC affiliated.
- ✉ 46 Moray Place, Edinburgh EH3 6BH
- ☎ 0131 225 6244   💻 www.eis.org.uk
- 👥 59,000

National Association of Headteachers (NAHT)
Main association representing the interests of headteachers. Independent.
- ✉ 1 Heath Square, Boltro Road, Haywards Heath, West Sussex RH16 1BL
- ☎ 01444 472472   💻 www.naht.org.uk
- 👥 30,000

National Association of School Masters/Union of Women Teachers (NASUWT)
Only TUC affiliated teachers' union representing teachers and headteachers in all parts of the UK.
- ✉ Hillscourt Education Centre, Rose Hill, Rednal, Birmingham B45 8RS
- ☎ 0121 453 6150   💻 www.nasuwt.org.uk
- 👥 250,000

National Union of Teachers (NUT)
Largest teaching union representing teachers and headteachers. TUC affiliated.
▭ Hamilton House, Mabledon Place, London WC1H 9BD
☎ 020 7388 6191   ▭ www.teachers.org.uk
👥 270,000

University and College Union (UCU)
Largest trade union and professional association for academics, lecturers, trainers, researchers and academic-related staff. TUC affiliated.
▭ 27 Britannia Street, London WC1X 9JP
☎ 020 7837 3636   ▭ www.ucu.org.uk
👥 120,000

Voice Formerly the Professional Association of Teachers (PAT)
Independent trade union representing teachers, headteachers, lecturers, teaching assistants, technicians, administrators and support staff, in the public and private sectors.
▭ 2 St James' Court, Friar Gate, Derby DE1 1BT
☎ 01332 372 337   ▭ www.voicetheunion.org.uk
👥 35,000

Curriculum qualifications

England, Wales & Northern Ireland
SAT	Statutory Assessment Tasks
GCSE	General Certificate of Secondary Education
BTEC	Business & Technician Education Council
NVQ	National Vocational Qualification
A Level	Advanced Level
A/S	Advanced Subsidiary Level

Scotland
Standard Grade	
Higher	
Advanced Higher	
SVQ	Scottish Vocational Qualification

NQF and SCQF

What is the NQF?
The **National Qualifications Framework (NQF)** and **Scottish Credit and Qualifications Framework (SCQF)** group together qualifications that place similar demands on learners.

NQF and SCQF equivalent qualifications

NQF Level	Qualifications	Vocational Qualifications
1	GCSE (grades D–G)	BTEC Introductory Diploma
		NVQ
2	GCSEs (grades A*–C)	BTEC First Diploma
		NVQ
3	A level	BTEC Diploma
	International Baccalaureate	BTEC National

SCQF Level	Qualification	Vocational Qualification
3	Foundation Standard Grade	
4	General Standard Grade	SVQ1
5	Credit Standard Grade	SVQ2
6	Higher	SVQ3
7	Advanced Higher	

Subject associations

Association for Science Education
College Lane, Hatfield, Hertfordshire AL10 9AA
☎ 01707 283000   www.ase.org.uk

Association for Teachers of Mathematics
Unit 7 Prime Industrial Park, Shaftesbury Street, Derby DE23 8YB
☎ 01332 346599   www.atm.org.uk

Centre for Information on Language Teaching and Research
3rd Floor, 111 Westminster Bridge Road, London SE1 7HR
☎ 020 7379 5101   www.cilt.org.uk

Economics and Business Studies Association (EBEA)
The Forum, 277 London Road, Burgess Hill RH15 9QU
☎ 01444 240150   www.ebea.org.uk

Geographical Association
160 Solly Street, Sheffield S1 4BF
☎ 0114 296 0088   www.geography.org.uk

Historical Association
59a Kennington Park Road, London SE11 4JH
☎ 020 7735 3901   www.history.org.uk

National Association for Advisors and Inspectors in Design and Technology

⌨ 68 Brookfield Crescent, Hampsthwaite, Harrogate, North Yorkshire HG3 2EE

☎ www.naaidt.org.uk

National Association for the Teaching of English (NATE)

⌨ 50 Broadfield Road, Sheffield, South Yorkshire S8 0XJ

☎ 0114 255 5419   💻 www.nate.org.uk

RE Today

⌨ 1020 Bristol Road, Selly Oak, Birmingham B29 6LB

☎ 0121 472 4242   💻 www.retoday.org.uk

Exam boards

Assessment & Qualifications Alliance (AQA)

⌨ Guildford Office Stag Hill House, Guildford, Surrey GU2 7XJ
   Harrogate Office 31-33 Springfield Avenue, Harrogate, North Yorkshire HG1 2HW
   Manchester Office Devas Street, Manchester M15 6EX

☎ Guildford 01483 506 506
   Harrogate 01423 840 015
   Manchester 0161 953 1180 💻 www.aqa.org.uk

Northern Ireland Council for the Curriculum, Examination and Assessment (CCEA)

⌨ 29 Clarendon Road, Clarendon Dock, Belfast BT1 3BG

☎ 02890 261200   💻 www.ccea.org.uk

City & Guilds

⌨ 1 Giltspur Street, London EC1A 9DD

☎ 020 7294 2800   💻 www.cityandguilds.com

Edexcel

⌨ Edexcel Customer Service, One90 High Holborn, London WC1V 7BH.

☎ 0844 576 0025   💻 www.edexcel.org.uk

London Chamber of Commerce and Industry Examinations Board (LCCIEB)

☎ 08707 202909   💻 www.lccieb.com

Oxford, Cambridge and RSA Examinations (OCR)

⌨ 1 Hills Road, Cambridge CB1 2EU

☎ 01223 553 998   💻 www.ocr.org.uk

Scottish Qualifications Authority (SQA)
☐ The Optima Building, 58 Robertson Street, Glasgow G2 8DQ
☎ 0845 279 1000   💻 www.sqa.org.uk

Welsh Joint Education Committee (WJEC)
☐ 245 Western Avenue, Cardiff CF5 2YX
☎ 029 2026 5000   💻 www.wjec.co.uk

Media

General media

BBC News	www.bbc.co.uk/learning/subjects/schools
Daily Telegraph	www.telegraph.co.uk/education
Guardian	education.guardian.co.uk
Independent	www.independent.co.uk/news/education
Times	www.timesonline.co.uk/tol/life_and_style/education
TES	www.tes.co.uk

Teachers TV

Freesat	650
Freeview	88
Sky	880
Tiscali TV	845
Virgin TV	240

Lesson planning

What is a learning style?

A learning style is the method of educating which best suits an individual. Teachers are encouraged to assess and adapt to the learning styles of their pupils. Common learning style definitions are shown below.

Auditory: learning occurs through hearing the spoken word.
Kinesthetic: learning occurs through doing and interacting.
Visual: learning occurs through looking at images, demonstrations and body language

Assessment

Formative
Teachers use their assessments (observation, homework, discussion etc) to adapt teaching and learning to meet student needs. Characterised as assessment for learning.

Summative
Students sit a test to assess their progress over a given period. Characterised as assessment of learning.

Inclusion – SEN and other barriers to learning

What do we mean by SEN pupils?
The DCSF defines students with **special educational needs (SEN)** as having 'learning difficulties or disabilities which make it harder for them to learn or access education than most other children of the same age'. School **special educational needs coordinators (SENCO)** are responsible for coordinating SEN provision within a school.

Attention deficit (hyperactivity) disorder (ADHD)
Students have difficulty focusing on a specific task. Easily distracted, they have a very short attention span and have trouble commencing work. Those with hyperactivity may act impulsively and erratically.

Autistic spectrum disorder (ASD)
Students share three main areas of difficulty: i) social communication; ii) social interaction; and iii) social imagination. The condition affects students in different ways, hence use of the word 'spectrum'.

Asperger's syndrome
Form of autism associated with more intellectually-able individuals.

Dyscalculia
Students have difficulty acquiring mathematical skills. They may have difficulty understanding simple number concepts and lack an intuitive grasp of numbers.

Dyslexia

Students have a marked and persistent difficulty in learning to read, write and spell. They may have poor reading comprehension, handwriting and punctuation skills.

Dyspraxia

Students are affected by an impairment or immaturity of the organisation of movement and often appear clumsy. They may have poor balance and coordination. Their articulation may also be immature and their language late to develop.

English as an additional language (EAL)/English as a secondary language (ESL)

Students whose main language at home (mother tongue) is a language other than English.

Emotional/behavioural disorder (EBD)

Students' behaviour provides a barrier to their learning despite implementation of effective school behaviour policy.

Hearing impairment (HI)

Students with a hearing impairment range from those with mild hearing loss to those who are profoundly deaf.

Individual education plan (IEP)

Document setting out additional support and strategies provided to meet the needs of a student with learning difficulties.

Moderate learning difficulty (MLD)

In comparison with their peers, students have much greater difficulty acquiring basic literacy and numeracy skills and in understanding concepts. Other difficulties include low self-esteem, low levels of concentration and underdeveloped social skills.

Multi-sensory impairment (MSI)

Students have a combination of visual and hearing difficulties. They may also have additional disabilities.

Physical disability (PD)

Students with a visual, mobility or orthopaedic impairment that impacts on their ability to access the curriculum.

Profound and multiple learning difficulty (PMLD)
In addition to very severe learning difficulties, students have other significant difficulties, such as physical disabilities, sensory impairment or a severe medical condition.

Severe learning difficulty (SLD)
Students have significant intellectual or cognitive impairments. This has a major effect on their ability to participate in the school curriculum without support.

Specific learning difficulty (SpLD)
Umbrella term used to cover a range of difficulties including dyslexia, dyscalculia and dyspraxia.

National SEN Associations

British Dyslexia Association
▤ Unit 8, Bracknell Beeches, Old Bracknell Lane, Bracknell RG12 7BW
☎ 0845 251 9002   www.bdadyslexia.org.uk

National Attention Deficit Disorder Information and Support Service
▤ P.O. Box 340 Edgware, Middlesex HA8 9HL
☎ 020 8952 2800   💻 www.addiss.co.uk

National Association for Language Development in the Curriculum
▤ Serif House, 10 Dudley Street, Luton LU2 0NT
☎ 01582 724724   💻 www.naldic.org.uk

National Autistic Society
▤ 393 City Road, London EC1V 1NG
☎ 020 7833 2299   💻 www.autism.org.uk

National Association for Special Educational Needs
▤ Nasen House, Amber Business Village, Amber Close, Amington, Tamworth, Staffordshire B77 4RP
☎ 01827 311500   💻 www.nasen.org.uk

Dyspraxia Foundation
▤ West Alley, Hitchin, Hertfordshire SG5 1EG
☎ 01462 454 986   💻 www.dyspraxiafoundation.org.uk

Royal National Institute for the Deaf
▤ 19-23 Featherstone Street, London EC1Y 8SL
☎ 0808 808 0123   💻 www.rnid.org.uk

Lesson plans

What should be included?

Many schools and universities have their own recommended lesson plan format. The suggested structure below provides a possible structure and key areas of content.

Teacher		Date		Subject	
Class		No. Pupils		Ability/Level	
		No. SEN Pupils		LSA Support	Y/N

Context	An introduction to... /Builds on material covered in a previous lesson... A cooperative/challenging class... strategies employed include ...		
Aim	Why do we ... What is the link between...		
Objectives	Understand key features of... Learn how to...		
Outcomes	Write down five facts about... Identify the key features of ...		**Keywords**
Structure		Teaching Activity	Pupil Activities
	Starter		Work in pairs
			Recall previous lesson
	Main Body		Complete exercise
			Work in pairs
	Plenary		Write down
			Discuss

Differentiation	Extension questions Peer support		
Assessment	Teacher led Q&A – targeted and open questions Marking books		
Resources	Text books, PowerPoint		
LSA Support	Focus on pupil x Circulate among all pupils		
SEN Pupils	Name	Condition	Strategy
		Dyslexia	Keywords on board LSA help writing h/w

Other useful websites

Site name:	A to Z of School Leadership and Management
Description:	Advice on legislation concerning schools, and guidance on a range of school-management issues.
URL:	www.teachernet.gov.uk/atoz

Site name:	Addresses of LAs in England with websites
Description:	A comprehensive list of LA contacts, news, information and communications from the DCSF.
URL:	www.dfes.gov.uk/localauthorities

Site name:	Advanced Skills Teachers
Description:	Information from Teachernet for teachers who wish to apply.
URL:	www.teachernet.gov.uk/professionaldevelopment/opportu-nities/ast

Site name:	BBC Key Stage 2 Revisewise bitesize revision
Description:	Revision work for Key Stage 2 students in English, mathematics and science from the BBC Education website.
URL:	www.bbc.co.uk/schools/revisewise

Site name:	BECTA – British Educational Communities and Technology Agency
Description:	The UK government's leading agency for information and communications technology (ICT) in education.
URL:	www.becta.org.uk

Site name:	Behaviour and Attendance
Description:	Information about the government's programme to improve pupil behaviour and attendance.
URL:	www.dfes.gov.uk/behaviourandattendance/index.cfm

Site name:	Birmingham Grid for Learning
Description:	The public portal contains resources and links for learners, teachers, parents and administrators.
URL:	www.bgfl.org/bgfl/

Site name:	Building Bridges
Description:	Information on the Independent/State School Partnerships Grant Scheme, set up to encourage collaborative working between independent and maintained schools.
URL:	www.dfes.gov.uk/buildingbridges

Site name:	CEGNET
Description:	Careers education website from the Connexions Service National Unit for schools and colleges and their partners.
URL:	www.cegnet.co.uk

Site name:	Children and Young People's Unit
Description:	The website of the government unit for the better coordination of policies and services for children.
URL:	www.allchildrenni.gov.uk/

Site name:	Choice
Description:	First online course prospectus for 14- to 19-year-olds in London. Includes a free searchable directory of over 25,000 courses with clear details of all the learning opportunities open to young people.
URL:	www.yourlondon.gov.uk/choice

Site name:	Citizenship
Description:	The DCSF citizenship website. Includes schemes of work and teaching resources, plus articles and information from assessment to whole-school issues.
URL:	www.dfes.gov.uk/citizenship

Site name:	Code of Practice on LA-School Relations
Description:	Link to a downloadable version of the code, providing statutory guidance on how to raise standards.
URL:	www.dfes.gov.uk/lea

Site name:	Connecting Voices (COVO)
Description:	A Southwark-based charity delivering services that address conflict, disaffection and underachievement in education and the workplace.
URL:	www.covo.org.uk

Site name:	Connexions
Description:	Guidance and support for 13- to 19-year-olds in all areas of life.
URL:	www.connexions.gov.uk

Site name:	Curriculum Online
Description:	A comprehensive catalogue of digital learning resources for the National Curriculum for England.
URL:	www.curriculumonline.gov.uk

Site name: Don't Suffer in Silence
Description: Website showing pupils, their families and teachers how to tackle bullying problems.
URL: www.dfes.gov.uk/bullying

Site name: Education Protects
Description: A project funded by the DCSF aiming to help raise the educational achievements of children and young people in care.
URL: www.dfes.gov.uk/educationprotects

Site name: DCSF – Languages Strategy
Description: The Languages for Life website outlining the government's languages plans to transform language use and acquisition.
URL: www.dfes.gov.uk/ languagesstrategy/

Site name: Directgov
Description: Main portal for access to UK government services, including the latest, up-to-date public-service information.
URL: www.direct.gov.uk

Site name: Every Child Matters: Change for Children
Description: Useful materials and case studies to help understand and deliver the *Every Child Matters* agenda.
URL: www.everychildmatters.gov.uk

Site name: Fast Track
Description: Accelerated leadership development programme for new teachers.
URL: www.dfee.gov.uk/fasttrack

Site name: Global Gateway
Description: Information for the development of an international dimension in education. Including ideas for lesson plans, free downloadable resources, an area for young people and information on gap years.
URL: www.globalgateway.org

Site name: Go-Givers
Description: Site showing primary children what it means to be part of a caring society. Including case studies for assemblies, discussion activities and a range of resources ideal for teaching citizenship.
URL: www.gogivers.org

Site name:　　Homework: The Standards Site
Description:　Support for the development of independent learning skills andattitudes for successful lifelong learning.
URL:　　　　www.standards.dfes.gov.uk/homework

Site name:　　Key Stage 3: The Standards Site
Description:　Information on the KS3 curriculum standards.
URL:　　　　www.standards.dfee.gov.uk/keystage3

Site name:　　Learning and Skills Council
Description:　Information and guidance on further education, work-based training, entry to employment and modern apprenticeships.
URL:　　　　www.lsc.gov.uk

Site name:　　Learning and Skills Development Agency
Description:　National resource for the development of policy and practice in post-16 education and training.
URL:　　　　www.lsda.org.uk

Site name:　　LifeBytes
Description:　Website for 11–14 year olds providing facts and information about their health.
URL:　　　　www.lifebytes.gov.uk

Site name:　　Literacy: The Standards Site
Description:　Support for teachers and educational professionals to improve literacy in schools.
URL:　　　　www.standards.dfes.gov.uk/primary/literacy

Site name:　　National Vocational Qualifications
Description:　Information on NVQs and the career opportunities they provide.
URL:　　　　www.dfes.gov.uk/nvq

Site name:　　Numeracy: The Standards Site
Description:　Support for teachers and educational professionals to improve numeracy in schools.
URL:　　　　www.standards.dfes.gov.uk/primary/mathematics

Site name:　　Practical Research for Education
Description:　Online journal for education students, teachers and educa-tion lecturers. Includes: free articles, profile interviews with researchers and a forum to discuss educational research.
URL:　　　　www.pre-online.co.uk

Site name: Primary National Strategy
Description: Support from the DCSF for all aspects of primary teaching.
URL: www.standards.dfes.gov.uk/primary

Site name: Qualifications and Curriculum Authority (QCA)
Description: Website of the QCA, the governing body who maintain and develop the school curriculum and assessments and accredit and monitor qualifications.
URL: www.qca.org.uk

Site name: School Lookup
Description: Access to the DCSF EduBase database of all nurseries, schools and colleges in the UK.
URL: www.easea.co.uk

Site name: SEN
Description: Special Educational Needs page from Teachernet offering information on SEN, including materials for teachers, parents and other education professionals.
URL: www.dfes.gov.uk/sen

Site name: Standards Site
Description: Internet materials and services aiming to support and improve teacher ability and raise levels of achievement.
URL: www.standards.dfes.gov.uk

Site name: Teachernet
Description: Education website for teachers and school managers, setting the government standard for UK teachers and schools-related professions.
Including resources, lesson plans and assessment strategies.
URL: www.teachernet.gov.uk/

Site name: Teachers' Pension Scheme
Description: Information about the Teachers' Pensions Scheme for England and Wales.
URL: www.teacherspensions.co.uk/

Site name: Teacher Xpress
Description: Resources and links to educational websites covering every area of the curriculum.
URL: www.teacherxpress.com

Site name: Times Educational Supplement
Description: Jobs, resources and ideas for all teachers and people working in education. Resource Bank section includes a large section of resources for teachers by teachers.
URL: www.tes.co.uk

References

ATL	www.atl.org.uk
BBC.co.uk	www.bbc.co.uk/health/
British Dyslexia Association	www.bdadyslexia.org.uk
DCSF	www.dcsf.gov.uk
Directgov	www.direct.gov.uk
Educational Resources.co.uk	www.educationalresources.co.uk
GTC England	www.gtce.org.uk
GTC Northern Ireland	www.gtcni.org.uk
GTTR	www.gttr.ac.uk
Info Scotland: Teaching in Scotland	www.teachinginscotland.com
NASUWT	www.nasuwt.org.uk
National Autistic Society	www.autism.org.uk
NUT	www.teachers.org.uk
Scottish Credit and Qualifications Network	www.scqf.org.uk
Scottish Executive Education Department	www.scotland.gov.uk/Topics/Education
Teachernet	www.teachernet.gov.uk
EIS	www.eis.org.uk
TDA	www.tda.gov.uk
TUC	www.tuc.org.uk
UCU	www.ucu.org.uk
Voice	www.voicetheunion.org.uk

Index